THE PRINT CASEBOOKS

FIRST ANNUAL EDITION

THE BEST IN COVERS

Conceived by
Martin Fox

Text and Introduction by
Nicholas Polites

Published by
RC Publications, Inc.
Washington, D.C.

Published by RC Publications, Inc., 6400 Goldsboro Road NW, Washington, D.C. 20034

Manufactured in U.S.A.
First Printing 1975

THE PRINT CASEBOOKS/FIRST ANNUAL EDITION/THE BEST IN COVERS
Library of Congress Catalog Card Number 75-12391
ISBN 0-915734-03-6

THE PRINT CASEBOOKS/FIRST ANNUAL EDITION
Complete 6-Volume Set
ISBN 0-915734-07-9

RC PUBLICATIONS
President and Publisher: Robert Cadel
Vice-President and Editorial Director: Martin Fox
Editor: Joel G. Cahn
Art Director/Designer: Andrew P. Kner
Associate Art Director: Rose M. DeNeve
Title Page Illustration: Isadore Seltzer

INTRODUCTION

There are lots of ways of looking at covers. One magazine editor was always to be heard intoning around deadline time, "Remember, a cover is our face to the world."

Covers are that, but they are something more besides, as this Casebook makes plentifully apparent. Their purpose is basically twofold: to communicate what's inside in a legible, informative way, and beyond that, to convey something of the character and essence of the contents. And because most covers exist in the competitive environment of newsstands, bookstores and record shops, they usually have to make their point with some degree of immediacy and impact.

Covers therefore tend to function as miniature posters. Some have a more posterish quality than others. Record jackets especially are often designed either to fold out into posters or to lend themselves to blow-up for promotional purposes. But even smaller formats, like book jackets or paperbacks, are also deliberately designed on the poster model.

Since a large part of human experience is captured in books, magazines and records, it's hardly surprising that covers exhibit a dramatic range in style and approach. This leaves the subject of cover design open to widespread observation, insight and generalization of the broadest sort. For this reason, it is more useful to approach the subject from a specific point of view.

Comparing covers by type, one can note right off that book covers look different from

magazine covers, and both look different from record jackets. Nevertheless, broad-scale comparisons pose problems. Can one avoid glibness in sorting out *The Letters of John Keats* and *The Case of the Elevator Duck,* on the one side, and comparing them with *Sun Ra's Fate in a Pleasant Mood,* on the other?

The answer is a cautious yes. There are generalizations to be made, stemming primarily from the nature of the different media themselves, and the audiences which they address.

Books have a relatively long shelf life, and even paperbacks are likely to become permanent possessions, part of one's household. Book covers consequently tend to be more conservative and serious in approach than magazine and record album covers. They are also sometimes more complex, because a book cover often has two lives—a bookstore life and an afterlife. In the bookstore its purpose is to attract the reader, and to reflect some image of the subject matter or literary quality of the work. On another level, the artwork and design often contain elements that have no specific meaning to the buyer until after he's read the book. While record and magazine covers may share that characteristic, they usually do so to a far less significant extent.

Magazines are more direct, straightforward and—the quotation marks are used advisedly—"simple." Journalism is by definition an ephemeral thing, and most magazines and Sunday supplements have to compete in that toughest, shrillest and most aggressive of all marketplaces,

the newsstand. As a result, covers tend to be more news-oriented, and more sensational. They often come on with a strongly assertive approach, making their point with an immediate impact. It is always a matter of degree, of course, for there are covers which have a softer approach, depending on the subject—for example, the Ms. cover on the movies, which evokes nostalgia.

Records are a case apart. For one thing, the jacket covers are, quite literally, packages, in that they contain and protect the product. Physically, they are separate from the things contained—anonymous black discs distinguishable only by their labels—so that from the very start of the design process they are often thought about in a less literal fashion than either magazines or books. Even more important, the buying audience for records is generally likely to be younger, trendier, more venturesome and responsive to innovative trends than book and magazine consumers. Music is also generally regarded, rightly or not — always with the exception of Bach, the strict contrapuntalists and polyphonists—as a freer and looser art form than writing. Record album artwork is consequently less stringent, less restricted to literal reference to its subject. Finally, the physical format of record jackets (square and large) is more permissive than most book or magazine covers, and is usually exceeded in size only by tabloid magazines and Sunday supplements. Thus it is not unusual to find album covers which have little direct tie-in with the recordings they contain.

By contrast, book and magazine covers are almost always selected or commissioned to relate to something specific in the subject matter or lead story, or to make one obvious point with compelling impact.

The covers shown in this Casebook were judged on the basis of total design. The emphasis was on the relationship of type and art and their appropriateness to the book, magazine or record, not on pretty pictures or immediate impact.

Four of the jurors readily admitted that they were looking for the unusual, the innovative, the fresh idea. The dirty word of the day was "rip-off." As Isadore Seltzer remarked: "If it's well done, but reminiscent of someone else's work, I feel annoyed. I feel it's lacking in its original statement."

Frank Metz sought originality, along with a high degree of professionalism. "But that again is part of what originality really means. The whole scope of the judging is to make an assessment of what is original, well-designed, well-printed. In short, to come up with the high spots of given areas of contemporary graphics."

For Ruth Ansel, the search was "for what is courageous, the design that is willing to take a risk. That's what really interests me. The risks are worth the gamble as long as you're not indulging your ego."

Seltzer further noted the subjectiveness of the judging process: "I like a piece, or respond to a piece, if it stimulates me esthetically. Not just that I find it pleasing—in some ways it can even be abrasive. It should have a strong feeling which reflects the material it's supposed to reflect, and parallels it. If there's a harmony between what I'm experiencing and what it's supposed to do, then I think it's been successful."

But Roger Jellinek, editor-in-chief of a major publishing house, and the only non-art director, non-designer in the group, found himself dissenting strongly from the other jurors. "Most of the art directors were looking for a breakthrough in design, so they were rarely surprised by what they saw, and most of the covers looked to them like repeats of ideas they already were aware of. Consequently, they were generally harsher than I was, or focused on a detail that was new, and ignored the general failure of communication in the jackets."

Jellinek explained that he was concerned primarily with psychology at point of contact, when a person first sees or handles the book. "The reader or consumer has prejudices or preconceptions. Tasks given to the book covers vary from reassuring the customer that what he is going to read is fresh, interesting, curious, new, to exploiting an established genre in a skillful or professional way."

Among the general comments offered by the jurors on the Casebook cover entries:

Ansel: "I think the whole level of graphic design in general has fallen off from its original kind of renaissance during the fifties and sixties, and I see it reflected in the entries. There were some very wonderful things, and some very mediocre things. But there wasn't enough top-level work to give me the sense that the best graphic design was being done. Most of what gets published falls someplace in the middle. Except that what used to be the middle was much higher than what it is now. Or at least on a more provocative level. The designers took more risks. Now, everybody's playing it safe. The originality really shows through when it's there, but it's lonely. It doesn't have the kind of camaraderie and the company that it used to have. I think everyone's been affected by the recession."

Seltzer: "Most of the entries, particularly the records, were surprisingly limited and, I would say, poor. There seemed to be plenty of books, and they were all right. But there were whole segments of the field that didn't seem to respond—the magazines, for instance. It was a bit disappointing that there wasn't a broader range to pick from."

Kner: "I think the technical quality of the entries is quite high." But then, agreeing with Ansel: "I think that people are playing it somewhat safe. Very rarely did I feel, 'Wow! That's really a fantastic graphic statement.' I always felt, 'That's nice, it's competent.' People seem to be holding back somehow. It's hard to get one's teeth into any kind of emerging, new way of doing things. There were a lot of covers which were funky, but they weren't really as funky as the stuff in the late sixties. The wildness, the freedom of the sixties affected everything, and maybe it loosened up some of the tighter kinds of things. But now everything is sliding toward the center." —Nicholas Polites

Roger Jellinek

Jellinek has been editor-in-chief of Quadrangle/The New York Times Book Company since January, 1974. He joined the New York Times Book Review as an editor in 1966, becoming assistant editor in 1970. Before that he worked for Random House and Walker & Company. British-born, he was educated at Cambridge University and came to the U.S. on a two-year Mellon Fellowship to Yale, studying politics and international relations during his first year, and spending the second year in the School of Architecture.

Nicholas Polites

Nicholas Polites is a writer, consultant and teacher. He was editor of the magazine Environment/Planning and Design from 1968 to 1971. Later he was a consulting and contributing editor to Saturday Review, and news editor of Architectural Forum. He has consulted with private and non-profit organizations, including Herman Miller, Inc., the Cooper-Hewitt National Museum of Design, and Walter Dorwin Teague Associates, Inc.

Ruth Ansel

Ruth Ansel has been art director of the New York Times Sunday Magazine for the past year. Before that she was art director of Harper's Bazaar for 10 years. She has had one-year stints as art director of Columbia Records, and of Scali, McCabe, Sloves, Inc. She also had a one-year stint at McCall's magazine as assistant art director. In addition to her regular duties, she has done free-lance assignments designing logos, letterheads, announcements, posters, calendars, books and book jackets, including *The Tiffany Touch* (Random House), *A Word to the Wives* (Knopf), and *Alice in Wonderland* (Dutton). While working in Paris she created experimental fashion film concepts.

Frank Metz

Metz is a vice president and art director of the trade division of Simon & Schuster. Since 1957 his responsibilities have included all paperback covers, illustrations and book jackets. He is also a painter and has had six one-man shows. His work appears in many public and private collections throughout the U.S. Metz was born in Philadelphia, where he attended the Philadelphia College of Art.

Isadore Seltzer

Seltzer, one of America's foremost illustrator/designers, lives and works in New York. Born in St. Louis, he moved to Los Angeles after high school and entered Los Angeles City College. Later, he studied at Chouinard Art Institute and the Art Center School. After free-lancing in Los Angeles for four years, he came to New York and joined Push Pin Studios, where he remained for five years before returning to free-lance work. He has won numerous prizes in graphic arts shows, and has been represented in group shows in Paris, London, Tokyo and Milan.

Andrew Kner

Since 1970, Kner has been art director of the promotion department of the New York Times, which he joined in 1969 as art director of the Sunday Book Review. Before that he was promotion and advertising art director of Esquire, Inc., and prior to that, assistant promotion art director at Look magazine. He has also worked as a designer for the book division of Time, Inc., and Architectural Forum. He has won awards from the Art Directors Club of New York, the Art Directors Club of Chicago, AIGA, Society of Illustrators and Society of Publication Designers. Born in Hungary, Kner is a member of the ninth generation of his family to work in design. He came to the U.S. at the age of five, and grew up in Chicago. He received his B.A. at Yale in 1957, and an M.F.A. in 1959. In addition to his work for the Times, he serves as art director of PRINT magazine.

The 90 covers shown and discussed in this Casebook were selected through a juried competition. Published during calendar year 1974, they include book, magazine and record album covers.

INDEX

Clients/Publishers/ Record Companies

Magazines/Book Titles/ Album Titles

Cage a Man

A good cover is more apt to result when art director and illustrator are involved in a project from the start, and when both are open to suggestion. This was the case with *Cage a Man*, a sci-fi thriller about lobster-like creatures on an alien planet. The art director, Bruce Green, suggested a cover design with lobster men predominating, but he also welcomed suggestions.

The illustrator accepted the initial suggestion, but proposed an alternative to just a front cover illustration: the idea of the back view of the jacket. The art director accepted, and the initial design solution was altered to accommodate the second illustration, showing the lobster man with all the science fiction gimmicks on his back.

Besides having an enjoyable project to work with, the illustrator liked being able to use both sides of the dust jacket. The book was sold through stores and through a book club, for which the lobster image was used in an advance announcement brochure.

Publisher: Doubleday, Inc.
Art director: Bruce Green
Designer/illustrator: Gary Viskupic
Copywriter: Dave Watson

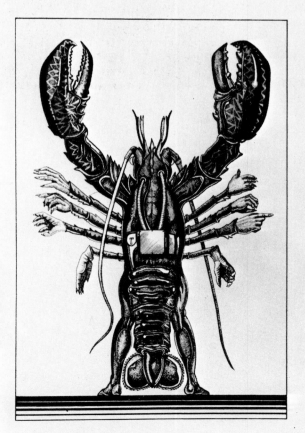
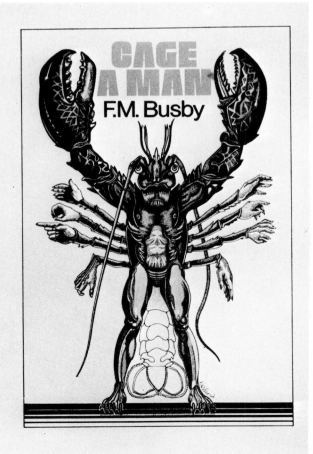

Nelson
Doubleday

The illustration for this jazz record album had originally been intended for the Bessie Smith series on Columbia, but it had not worked out. When the assignment for *Mr. Jones* came along, no original design requirements were set, nor was any information supplied besides the title. However, designer Lloyd Ziff remembered having seen the sketch in the illustrator's studio in New York some years earlier. The two of them discussed using it for this record jacket, and with a few alterations it was made to work. The cover continues the tradition of strong graphic solutions established in previous Elvin Jones albums, and has since won several awards.

Client: Blue Note Records (United Artists Records)
Art director: Mike Salisbury
Design firm: United Artists Art Dept., Los Angeles
Designer: Lloyd Ziff
Illustrator: Philip Hays

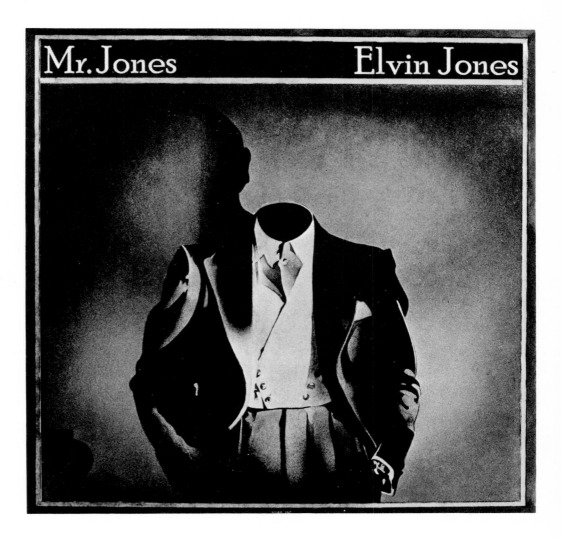

From the beginning of the
assignment designer and art
director wanted to find a fresh
approach to Westerns by getting
an 1890s pulp look. For
authenticity, they decided to use
a painting by the famous
Western painter Frederic
Remington. The main problem
became one of finding the right
Remington painting for the
cover, and acquiring
reproduction rights. "These
problems were dealt with
through lots of research, leg
work, correspondence and
phone calls," says the art
director. The painting appearing
on the cover is entitled, simply,
"Cowboy"; it was painted
around 1890.

Publisher: Dell Publishing
Art director: Bruce W. Hall
Designer: Richard Rossiter
Illustrator: Frederic Remington
Copywriter: John M. Boswell

A Money cover may begin with an idea from a writer, or an editor, or the art department, but whatever the source, it's always discussed in detail at a meeting attended by art director, managing editor, writer, researcher, and the senior editor responsible for the cover story. The meeting's purpose is to encourage an interplay of ideas so that final concept will accurately reflect the story. Once the concept is established, the cover will usually be completed in one or two weeks.

All three covers shown here reflect this well-thought-out approach. Though strong, they avoid sensationalism. The magazine's approach is to try to suggest a solution within a cover, or to show an important trend or development, rather than to portray a problem as either insoluble or generally hopeless.

The March 1974 issue appeared at a time when there were long gas lines that, it was generally predicted, would last through summer and fall. Some in-depth investigation by a staff writer, however, showed that the situation would improve by summer. The cover therefore became a poster-like rendition, using bold summer colors. But to contrast with the cover headline and to balance against any tendency toward over-optimism, a bit of skeptical graffiti were added to the highway sign.

For September 1974, a placid Grant Wood landscape painting of a traditional American scene was used to dramatize the change in American house-buying customs. Some alterations were made on the

MARCH 1974 75 CENTS

Money

Eight Underused Income Tax Savings
The Prospects for Women Returning to Work
Buying Stocks at Cut-Rate Commissions

FUEL-FC

Vacation driving:
There'll be gas enough to get there

cover so that it adheres more closely to the Grant Wood painting on which it was based. The result was a faithful rendition of the original painting, with the exception of the new kind of homebuilding depicted on the cover. There was a technical problem in adjusting a basically horizontal composition to a vertical cover, but that was solved by placing it at the bottom, and using the top for logo and type.

A powerful graphic image made the November 1974 cover highly visible on the newsstands. A photograph of the same subject was initially considered, but it was rejected in favor of the painting, which could be made bolder by showing the shirt made of armor plating.

This dramatic concept was established in the original story conference and carried through with only the slightest changes. When the painting was about three-quarters completed, the art director and illustrator agreed that the collar should be made whiter and the armor plating even bolder. So that the painting could be run in four-color to most accurately reproduce the original, the logo was printed in a fifth color. a fifth color.

Art director Peter Rauch considers this one of the magazine's most surrealistic covers, possibly, he says "because of the exaggeration of the peril to the subject and the protection inherent in his job."

Money

SEPTEMBER 1974 75 CENTS

Should You Buy Gold?
Diagnosing Your Health Insurance
Higher Fi for Lower Prices

INFLATION CLOSES IN ON THE ONE-FAMILY HOUSE

Publisher: Time, Inc.
Art director: Peter Rauch
March 1974:
Designer: Peter Rauch
Illustrator: Tom Upshur
Copywriter: William Rukeyser
September 1974:
Designer: Robert Daniels
Illustrator: Robert Alcorn
Copywriter: Peter Bird Martin
November 1974:
Designer: Robert Dougherty
Illustrator: Roy Carruthers
Copywriter: William Rukeyser

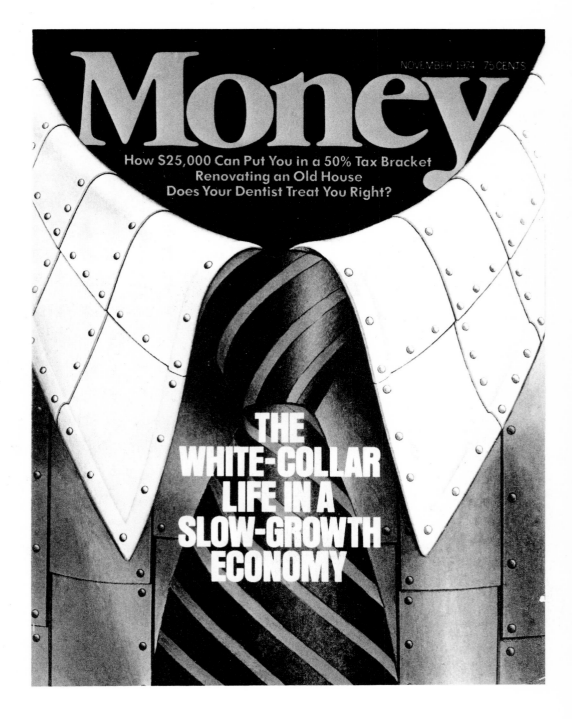

Lennart Nilsson's *Behold Man* is a book of spectacular photography of the human body, with striking blow-ups of details like human cells, nerve ganglia, intestinal linings that resemble weirdly extraterrestrial mountain ranges.

Since the book had been published in other countries, the art director was presented with imported jackets from Holland, Sweden, and other countries. None exhibited graphic excellence, in his opinion. Therefore, he and the designer decided to create an original cover using an interior book photo and the book title to create a contemporary, dynamic and legible solution. The cover was completed in ten days.

Publisher: Little, Brown and Co.
Art director: Char Lappan
Designer: John Renfer
Photographer: Lennart Nilsson

Romance Is on the Rise

Some assignments are more ideal than others. In this case, designer Ruth Ansel was given a demonstration record, a series of fine Richard Avedon color photographs, and *carte blanche* to come up with an album cover of her own devising.

Because she found Waite's singing style funky, Ansel wanted the album cover to reflect a mood of fun and sex, and to have what could be described as a "modern-nostalgia" look. She also wanted a visual idea that would take advantage of all the Avedon photographs.

The original requirements were changed in one important way. The color photos were converted to black-and-white, and hand-colored to achieve the desired look. "This was an unusual procedure," says Ansel, "but it worked."

Several different cover designs were tried, some without border, others with more than one large figure, and still others with many small figures all over the cover. The final choice—by consensus of the photographer and clients—also turned out to be the strongest poster and the freshest design visually. Except for minor cropping problems the final cover design came out exactly as originally intended.

Client: Paramour Records
Art director/designer: Ruth Ansel
Photographer: Richard Avedon
Copywriter: John Phillips

The conventional approach to doing a book cover about boxing is to take a single old photo of a boxer—or several photos—and present it with a typographic treatment of the title. Which is precisely what *In This Corner* scrupulously avoids.

The art director asked the illustrator to try to capture the feeling of a George Bellows boxing picture, and his first rough crayon pencil sketch was accepted immediately. The finished painting establishes a great sense of realism and nostalgia. The illustrator did all the lettering, which results in a beautifully integrated package that has far more interest than an old sepia photograph. Both author and editor were very excited with the finished cover.

This is one of the last assignments the late Roger Hane completed before his tragic death in 1974. He was brutally assaulted riding his bicycle in Central Park. That he was a young man who had already achieved much but hadn't even nearly reached the midpoint of his working career makes the tragedy all the more painful—and this cover all the more precious.

Publisher: Simon & Schuster
Art director: Frank Metz
Designer/illustrator: Roger Hane

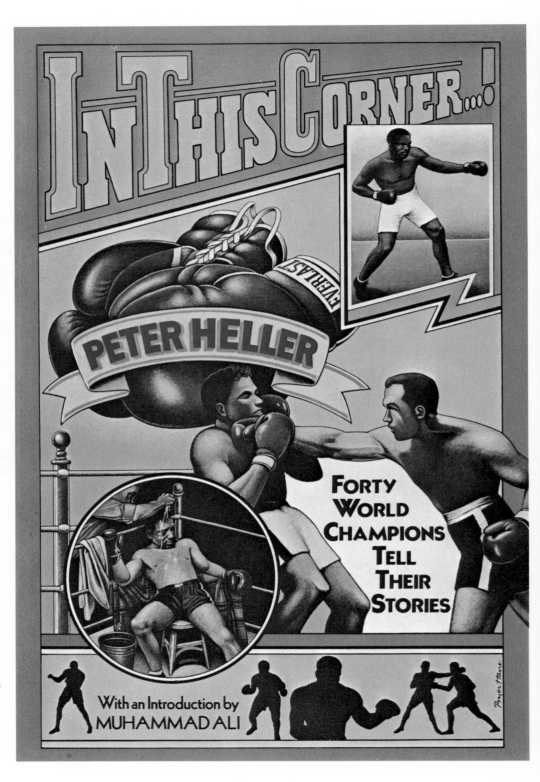

Scope is a veterinary magazine published as an external house organ by a major pharmaceutical company. Because of the nature of the journal, photographs inside are usually about "nuts and bolts" medical topics. Some are very gory. The tendency is therefore to keep the cover clean and well-designed. Even so, in this cover illustrating an article on canine spinal-cord diseases, the art director considered alternatives. One was to photograph an actual spinal column of a dog. Another layout used a photo of a dog suffering from a spinal disease.

Even before the final cover design was presented and approved, a photograph was taken of the ceramic dog with a red gel light focused on the spine. The photo was necessary to suggest the subtlety of this solution, which would have been difficult to convey in a sketch.

This approach of borrowing interest from a symbolic representation was immediately recognized as the best and most elegant one. It was readily accepted by the editor.

Publisher: Upjohn Co.
Art director: Bob Klunder
Design firm: Garrison, Jasper, Rose & Co., Inc., Indianapolis, IN
Designer: Bob Klunder
Photographer: Clarence Kirk
Copywriter: Dr. Alan J. Parker

veterinary

SCOPE

Diagnosis and Treatment of Canine Spinal Cord Disease

Variations of the Ocular Fundus of the Bovine Species

The prototype issue of Avant-Garde featured several pages on the art of Roy Carruthers, which made cover design merely a matter of selecting a painting from among several that would have strong possibilities. The particular one displayed here (titled "Miss Color Stat") was chosen for its exceptional graphic impact. It was originally commissioned by K&S Photo Labs in Chicago for use as a promotional poster. Using discordant elements and distorted shapes to create graphic tension, it is representative of much of Carruthers' best-known work, and an appropriate beginning for a popular arts and leisure tabloid whose penchant was for striking and unusual imagery.

Publisher: Avant-Garde Media, Inc.
Design firm: Lubalin Smith Carnase, Inc.
Art director/designer: Herb Lubalin
Illustrator: Roy Carruthers

Bike!

A bold design featuring a motorcycle that dominates both front and back of the cover jacket uses strong colors to create a surprisingly dynamic poster effect (given the size of the format). The back cover communicates the contents of the book in a very effective way. "Budgetary considerations always come into play with book jacket work because it is, of course, among the lowest paying design jobs," designer Mark Rubin remarks. "The only way, therefore, to make it worthwhile is to get the job in and out the door as quickly as possible. This means getting comps accepted on the first shot. It's not always possible, but we've done it about 80 per cent of the time."

This cover was produced without any problems. Time allotted for the comprehensive was approximately three weeks, with another two weeks for finished mechanical. Like many independent designers who work with client art directors, what this one found most satisfying about the assignment was the good professional and personal working relationship: "They make the design assignment a pleasure. They're professionals."

Publisher: Harper & Row
Art directors: Al Manso, Bob Cheney
Designer/illustrator: Mark Rubin

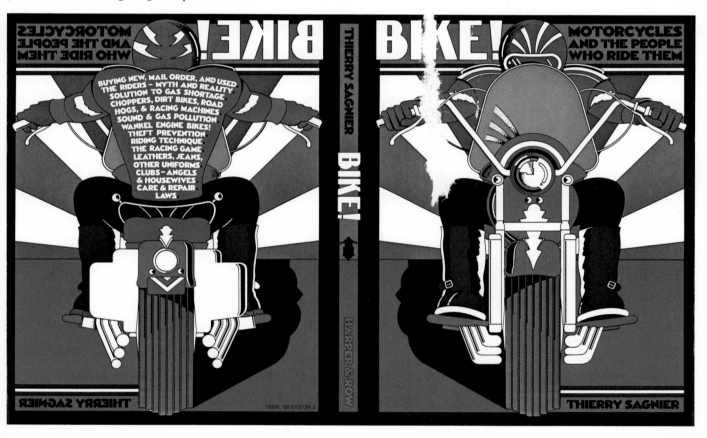

The cover for Astralsignal resulted from a close personal involvement between art director and all parties concerned with the making of the record. As a vice president of United Artists, art director Bob Cato often begins working with musicians and their producers during the recording sessions. In this case, he knew from the producers that the musician had taken a new direction. To overcome Gene Harris' image of "black artist," the album needed a strong name as well as a change in the look and the art to establish a contemporary image.

The producers wanted the title to connote something about sound and space. An interest in astrology led Cato to suggest "Astralsignal," which sounded properly mystical and spacey. The artwork follows the same theme, and proceeds from Cato's interest in spatial problems. The symbols suggest earth and space and ancient geometrical forms. The woman's figure and face come from a large aluminum sculpture created by Cato.

In most record jacket projects, the art director spends as much time with the artist as possible, to create a good rapport from which a satisfactory cover can evolve. Musicians sometimes find it hard to convey what kind of feeling the cover should evoke; visits to the studio, access to the work in progress, and time spent with the art director usually tend to make them more articulate.

This particular cover was created over a period of about four weeks. Initially it was to be a double-fold album, but the original idea of giving a full

account of the recording session did not come through, and thus it was made into a single jacket. Cato's first choice of paper, Kilmory, was not available, and Needlepoint was used instead.

Client: United Artists Records
Art director: Bob Cato
Design firm: United Artists Art Dept., Los Angeles
Designer/illustrator: Bob Cato
Photographer: Kenny Dorr

Wilhelm Reich Series

The main requirements for a paperback series of Wilhelm Reich books was that they have a family look and allow for the addition of new titles at a later date. The books are sold primarily in paperback psychology sections of bookshops. They also have a college text and reference orientation.

Several approaches were explored with rough initial tissues in the early design phase, including symbols (Fig. A), which didn't work because they clashed with the previous series and pure type (Fig. B), which seemed flat. The success of the approved solution was due partly to the unexpected discovery of a rare old newspaper photo of Reich as a young man in the Austrian army. The photo made possible a human interest approach with graphic impact, using large engraver's dots in three-color printing. The solution was also different enough from existing, similar books so that no confusion would arise.

The biggest problem was establishing color schemes, including color changes, for each title. 3M Color Keys helped to some extent. The printer exercised some freedom of choice in matching the comprehensive. Final adjustments were made in proofing.

Everything about the covers proved satisfying to the designer: subject matter, graphic challenge, discovering the almost unknown photograph, working to find interesting color combinations and ways to reproduce them. The fact that the jackets could be pushed beyond the range of elegant type handling or the direct information designs of most paperbacks—by combining graphic identity and human interest—is the most distinguishing characteristic of the series.

Publisher: Simon & Schuster/ Touchstone Books
Art director: Frank Metz
Designer: Robert Anthony

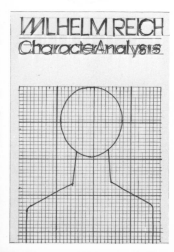

Sometimes the connection between a cover and the work inside is subtle or tenuous. When this is deliberate, a wholly different point of view about covers becomes the approach to design.

CTI Records is a small label that specializes in jazz. Since the company doesn't produce folk, rock, country or any other kind of music, it seeks label identification by presenting a solid front on cover style. Covers like *Canned Funk, Penny Arcade* and *Goodbye* use graphically exciting photography that is not necessarily related to the album's contents. In fact, some of the artwork plunges straight into the surreal and enigmatic.

The photography very often precedes the recording itself, so titles of the album often originate from the photography.

Typography is kept as simple and spare as possible in order not to interfere with the strong photos.

The company's policy is to work closely with a small group of photographers and to review their work periodically with an eye toward cover photographs. Sometimes a photographer is assigned to shoot a subject the art director has thought of and put in sketch form. But often, the photographer is shooting without any cover in mind.

Though the policy of using strong photography that doesn't necessarily relate to the album describes CTI's general approach, it is not always rigidly applied. An exception is *Keep Your Soul Together,* which is an attempt to build Freddy Hubbard as a personality by showing him, in an intriguing way, reclining on the red-lips sofa. The idea worked because Hubbard is considered a sex object among jazz enthusiasts.

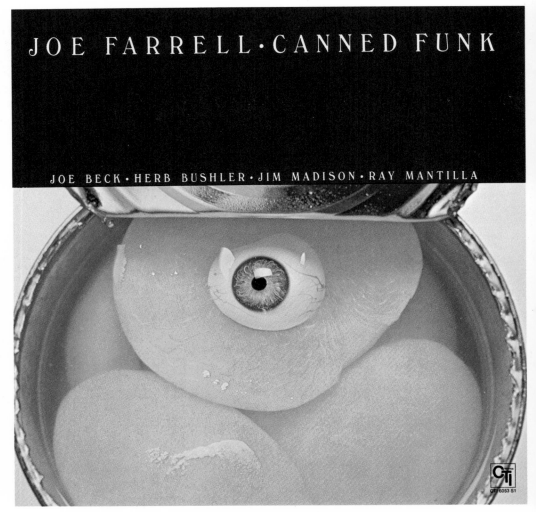

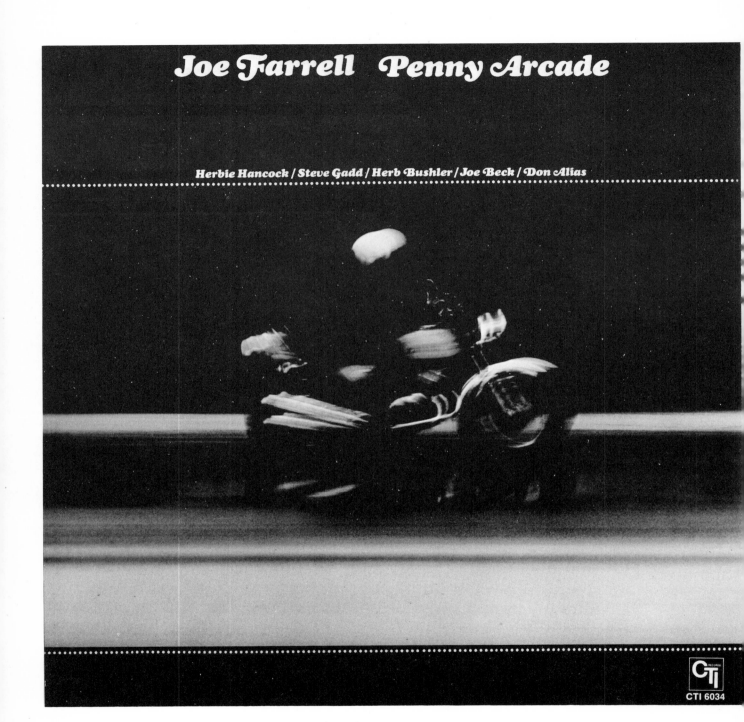

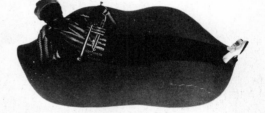

Client: CTI Records
Art director/designer: Bob Ciano
Photographer: Pete Turner
Copywriter: Creed Taylor

There's seldom anything subtle about New York magazine's covers. They are bright, aggressive, punchy, full of variety—a perfect newsstand counterpart of the brash competitive spirit that makes the city tick. Niceties like esthetics and technical perfection often get lost in the shuffle, but more important is that the covers are almost always entertaining and often funny, especially the ones about politics.

Cover ideas are usually generated by Walter Bernard and Milton Glaser from verbal or written outlines of a story. If an illustration is involved, a sketch of the idea may then be sent to an artist. From inception to completion, covers are done under rush deadlines, often as little as three or four days.

This was the precise procedure for both covers shown here.

The most satisfying aspect of the Nixon cover, according to Bernard, was "the hope that it would come true." The fine execution of the Kissinger sphinx by the illustrator contributed strongly to the concept's success.

What's Free in February
Does Wall Street Know a Bargain?
by Andrew Tobias

FEBRUARY POSTER-SIZE ENTERTAINMENT CALENDAR

50 CENTS · FEBRUARY 4, 1974

NEW YORK

Is Nixon Finally Going Under?

Why Things Are
Going to Get Worse
Before They Get Worse,
By Joseph Kraft

The Remarkable
Jaworski
Prosecution Team,
By Robert Daley

The Sinister Force
Entangling Al Haig,
By Evans
And Novak

Publisher: New York Magazine
Art directors: Walter Bernard, Milton
Glaser
Designer: Milton Glaser
Illustrators: David Wilcox ("Nixon"),
Melinda Bordelon ("Kissinger")

The World's Greatest Operettas

This two-record album of operetta hits could have been designed in the same format as any other two-record set, with separate front and back covers. But the designer wanted a solution that would give maximum visual impact, and the conventional approach was rejected as being too standard. Instead, front and back covers were designed as an integral unit; when opened, they can have further use as a poster.

All the important printed information had to be retained on the front half of the package so that the album could also work for display in record shelves. Apart from that there were no technical problems. Obtaining the final results with a different format became the most satisfying aspect of this project for the designer.

Client: RCA Records
Art director/designer: J.J. Stelmach
Design firm: RCA Art Dept. and Ralph Keefe Studios, New York
Illustrator: Richard Amsel
Copywriter: Nancy Swift

The problem in creating a cover for a book about an area in the California north was to suggest the diversity of its human, animal and plant life. The only information submitted was a photograph from the author of a typical locale. It was inadequate. The art director, designer and illustrator had previously worked out a scheme of pen-and-ink illustrations for the book's interior, in which captions were incorporated into banners as an integral part of the composition (see below). This became the take-off point for the jacket design.

The first approach consisted of a large framed version of the present cover illustration, with a simple banner at the head containing the title and author's name, hand-lettered in the inside style of the book's captions. Though the design suggested the rural, pastoral quality of the territory, it did not suggest the variety of life strongly enough to please the editorial department. It was then decided to reduce the size of the illustration and add a banner at the bottom with a lengthy blurb. The illustrator and designer worked out a system of including small spot drawings within the large banner, thus keeping it illustrative and distinct from the banner containing the title. The two banners are unified in style by the hand-lettering.

The final printed version was a one-color jacket that was attractive, saleable, and compatible in color, texture and flavor with the book's interior.

Publisher: Alfred A. Knopf (Random House, Inc.)
Art director: Betty Anderson
Designer: Earl Tidwell
Illustrator: Mark Livingston

Illustrations from inside book.

AMERICA'S GRAPHIC DESIGN MAGAZINE
JANUARY/FEBRUARY 1974
PRINT XXVIII:I

A PRINT cover tends to be quite important to the illustrator or designer invited to provide one, because the magazine is for and about graphic artists—the cover artist is talking to his peers. Covers are usually assigned to an individual whose work is being featured in a major portfolio in a particular issue, and he or she is free to relate the cover to a specific article in the issue or to ignore the contents entirely and either make a general state-of-the-art visual comment or a more personal state-of-the-artist one. In assigning the cover, art director Andrew Kner conceives his role as being to define what the magazine is and then let the cover artists express their feelings in their own way.

When Roy Carruthers was asked for a cover in conjunction with the publication of a portfolio of his work in PRINT, he decided to use a painting he was already working on for himself, which had a strong, simple image. Entitled ''The Triumph of Nature,'' it was the left panel of a large diptych (the right-hand panel being ''The Triumph of Science''). Carruthers describes how the cover evolved:

''I was hoping to have the painting completed in time, but a week before the deadline no end was in sight. So I decided to do a smaller version in watercolor, which was finally used for the cover. As it turned out, the original painting wasn't completed till several months later. I was very happy with the assignment, since it gave me the opportunity to reproduce one of my own personal pictures, without the usual restrictions of an illustration assignment.''

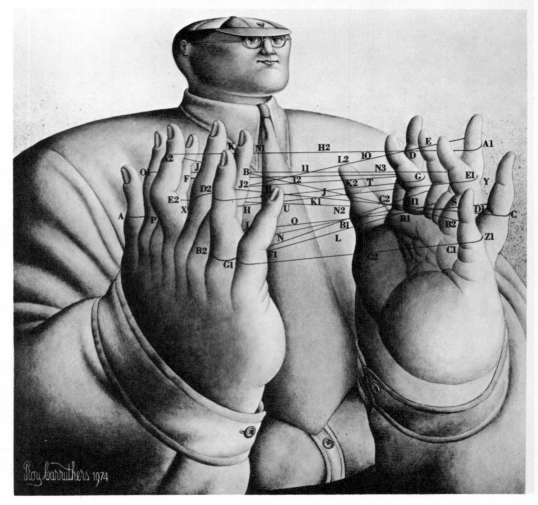

The National Lampoon cover is typical of what one might expect from the art directors of a humor magazine: a visual joke for art directors.

The cover was done in conjunction with a larger assignment—writing and producing an 8-page ''lampoon'' of the design field, a field which tends to take itself too seriously. The lampoon was scheduled to run back-to-back with an 8-page story on National Lampoon itself, and so the issue cover had to relate to both articles—one *by* and one *about* the Lampoon.

AMERICA'S GRAPHIC DESIGN MAGAZINE
JULY/AUGUST 1974
PRINT XXVIII:IV

Print

National Lampoon
Art Directing the Humor Magazine

While coming up with ideas to fill the 8-page lampoon section posed no problem, coming up with an appropriate cover idea was another matter entirely. "Ideas for the cover didn't flow like those for the article," states David Kaestle. "Then one day Doug Kenney, a Lampoon editor, wandered by, spent a couple of minutes listening to our overly intellectual attempts to come up with a symbol which would represent a common denominator among graphic designers, and then asked: 'Has every designer had the experience of slicing off a piece of his finger with a razor knife?' 'Is the Pope Catholic?' was our response—and his question became the solution.

"We didn't even need to give the image a funny twist—just put it on the cover, as is, in all its memorable horror. The idea itself dictated the specific treatment. Make it look just like it happened . . . as if preparation of the cover mechanical was just getting underway when the accident happened.

"Using PRINT's standard printed mechanical boards, we prepared several identical 'props'—logo in place, half-pasted repro for the cover line. Having a few back-ups would give us the flexibility to play a little with the stage blood at the shooting. Dick Frank, one of the most capable still-life photographers around, agreed to take the shot. Dick shot straight down on 8 by 10 film, using a large bank of strobes to get a good highlight off the blade's edge. The stage blood behaved beautifully and the back-up boards were never needed."

Publisher: RC Publications, Inc.
Art director: Andrew P. Kner
May/June 1974:
Illustrator: Roy Carruthers
July/August 1974:
Design firm: National Lampoon Art Department
Designers: David Kaestle, Michael Gross
Photographer: Dick Frank

The Missing White House Tapes

A very direct design concept is like a metaphor that gets to the heart of the matter with a swift stab. Nothing seems simpler, more obvious, or more effective.

When discussing how to package the White House tapes album, the art director and the copywriter came to the simple conclusion that they should literally "package" the tapes. Copy was written for funny postage and mailing stamps, such as "Ears Only," or "Electronically Rechanneled to Simulate the Truth."

Because the concept was so direct, the cover came in well under budget, though it was consistent in style with the usual National Lampoon product. Costs were merely those of a few rubber stamps, some string, and photography of the package. Producing the package itself took about one hour once the elements had been assembled. There were no sketches and no alterations.

Client: National Lampoon
Art director/designer: Michael Gross
Design firm: Pellegrini, Kaestle and Gross, Inc., New York
Photographer: R.G. Harris
Copywriter: Henry Beard

The cover of the study of Frantz Fanon—a key figure in the Algerian liberation movement—is itself a study in making the most from the least. The only material provided the art department was a very poor black-and-white photograph of the subject (below). The requirement was that the cover be attractive, that it have a quality look as opposed to a mass-market approach, and that it compete successfully in paperback bookstores.

Working with the blurred and out-of-focus photograph, the illustrator used a combination of photographic techniques and artwork (the color was added by hand) to achieve a very simple but powerful cover face. The border was conceived of as part of the illustration.

Publisher: Vintage Books (Random House, Inc.)
Art director/designer: Judith Loeser
Illustrator: Elias Dominguez

Rolling Stone's tabloid format, its heavy newsstand sales, and its young buying audience all tend to encourage mass-appeal covers: usually a news-style photograph of a celebrity in some striking or characteristic pose. The covers shown here depart from that norm.

The Bob Dylan cover was one of two covers commemorating Dylan's historic tour in 1974, the musical event of the year for Rolling Stone's audience. The first had followed the usual style; it was a news-style photograph of Dylan for a feature announcing the tour. For the second cover, however, a different feeling was wanted. Published while the tour was still in progress, the lead article focused on a deeper look at the significance of Dylan. To mark the shift of emphasis, a heroic but realistic image was sought rather than a reportorial photograph. A painting was commissioned from Paul Davis, which casts Dylan in an aura of darkness, prophecy, mystery. The client altered the painting by cropping and enlarging the head.

The "Ears Only" cover is the first purely typographic cover ever used for the magazine. Actually, the project was a two-color (red and black) cover on a special pull-out section of the magazine that was reused as a completely free supplement for distribution in hi-fi equipment stores. After arriving at the concept, art director Tony Lane experimented with several variations using a crude wood type of grotesque faces. The final result achieved what he calls "simplicity, its impact bordering on being crass without crossing over the line."

SM14170

ROLLING STONE ®

ISSUE NO. 156   MARCH 14, 1974   75¢ UK25p

The Poet's Poet
by Michael McClure

ROCK ME MAHARAJ JI
The Little Guru
Without A Prayer

UP FROM CBS
The Smothers Brothers
Slow Road Back

Publisher: Rolling Stone
Art director/designer: Mike Salisbury ("Dylan"), Tony Lane ("Ears Only")
Illustrator: Paul Davis ("Dylan")
Copywriter: Christine Doudna ("Ears Only")

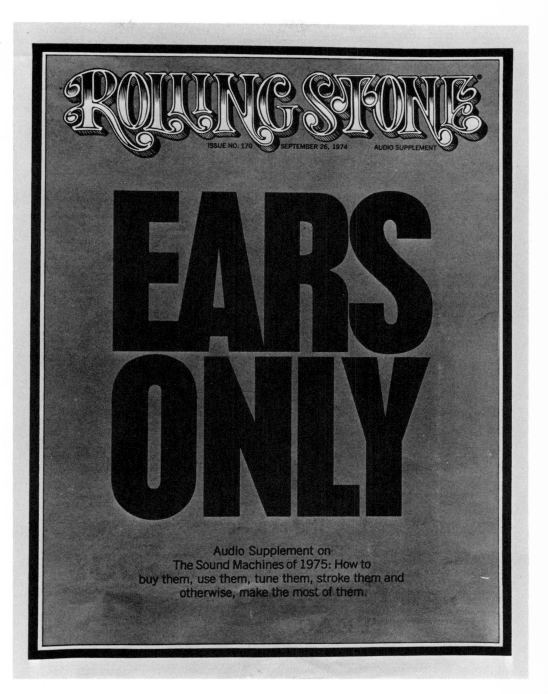

When a publisher issues a major title, there is more than just passing interest in its point-of-purchase appeal. The design may be reviewed by the sales manager, and sometimes by all the sales personnel.

The Last Dogfight was considered a major title by its publisher. While not restricting the dust jacket to any single approach, the art director, Louise Noble, suggested a Saturday Evening Post format evoking the 1940s to illustrator Wendell Minor, with the two main characters in the novel depicted on the cover.

Minor followed this approach and implemented the Post format by using strong type, flat-color background, and a panel illustration. He liked the result—an attractive and easily readable cover for good shelf exposure and maximum poster effect—and so did the art director and the author. The illustrator proceeded to final art and mechanical.

When the sales manager saw the cover, however, he objected to certain details. As a former World War II pilot, he questioned the positioning of the airplanes. But the illustrator refused to make changes on the basis of the sales manager's flying expertise, since the subject had been carefully researched and the illustration fit the manuscript description of the scene.

The art director then had to recommission the cover from another artist. Both covers were to be shown at an upcoming sales conference. When the date came, the original cover was accepted by popular vote of the salesmen.

The story ends happily. The book has sold three hardcover editions and is already into a new printing.

THE LAST DOGFIGHT
A NOVEL BY MARTIN CAIDIN

Publisher: Houghton Mifflin Co.
Art director: Louise Noble
Designer/illustrator: Wendell Minor
Copywriter: Austin Olney

Harper's typical cover style is a strong photograph and bold headlines that leap out at the newsstand buyer to attract his attention. This was the first issue of the magazine ever to use a collage on the cover.

The minstrel figure tightrope-walking over the collage of machine parts symbolizes the precariousness of the arts and humanities in a technological culture. Although the cover was readily accepted by the editors and proved a great *succès d'estime*, the issue didn't get the usual newsstand sales. Part of the disappointing results were attributed to the muted colors that were used (black type against a medium blue background). The next cover collage, according to art director Sheila Berger, will be much bolder.

Publisher: Harper's Magazine
Art director: Sheila Berger
Illustrator: Richard Mantel
Copywriter: Robert Shnayerson
(Editor)

Jerry Ford: Hail to the Commoner-in-Chief
Training Children to Cheat: The Soap Box Derby Scandal

02049

Harper's
Magazine

August 1974 $1.00

ON TRUSTING YOUR OWN PERCEPTIONS

Saul Bellow: Minstrels v. Machines

Murray Kempton: Truth v. "News"

Newsday's TV Magazine

A good design turns restriction to advantage. The assignment here was a cover on the rash of new television series featuring policewomen. The designer/illustrator began thinking of images and symbols that would graphically tell the story. The problem was making them fit the confines of the compact television book format (9¾" wide by 7¼" deep). The solution was to meld gun and woman into one image that summed up the TV emphasis on policewomen.

One technical problem arose. The original background color was a bit mottled. The editor suggested that the color be "flashed-in" at the plant. The idea worked, and the blemishes were eliminated.

Publisher: Newsday
Art director: Mike Killelea
Design firm: Newsday Editorial Art Department
Designer/illustrator: Gary Viskupic
Copywriter: Tony Gentile

The John Collier Reader

This is actually the second cover created for this book. Though it satisfied the designer, Larry Ratzkin, because of its elegance and modern classicism, his first solution (below), a drawing of a monkey sitting and reading *The John Collier Reader,* is still the one he prefers. The first idea was based on Collier's "Monkey Wife," which is told from the point of view of a monkey. It was rejected by the client, probably because it was too clever.

The four faces which appear on the printed cover were found in a book on the Great Exhibition of 1851 (Crystal Palace, London), and perfectly express what the designer felt about Collier's writing. This solution was readily accepted without changes by the client.

Publisher: Alfred A. Knopf (Random House, Inc.)
Art director: Robert D. Scudellari
Designer: Lawrence Ratzkin

The John Collier Reader

rapier-pointed tales
of fate, evil, and
retribution from
one of the
finest storytellers
of our time,
together with
the full text of
his incomparable novel,
His Monkey Wife

**Introduction by
Anthony Burgess**

The covers for American
Heritage college texts have
become an object lesson in how
to design a continuing series
(this one has gone on for a
dozen years). The books all fall
within the area of American
history and sociology, but
subjects vary widely and the
time framework ranges from
before the Revolution to the
current day.

Because budgets are low, and
because the designer is in one
city, the publisher in another,
and the printer elsewhere, the
designer strives for simplicity.
Art is kept rigidly to a square.
Type style is constant and is
treated in a fairly classical
manner. Within the outline of a
4½″ by 4½″ square, however,
art and color can vary widely,
depending on subject matter of
the text.

For the designer, the most
gratifying aspect in his
relationship with the client has
been trying to keep up
standards set 12 years ago for a
series that was not expected to
go on so long (he has designed
approximately 50 titles to date).
Fortunately, the format that was
established was flexible and
timeless enough to
accommodate new titles and
visuals without becoming dated.

Publisher: Bobbs-Merrill Co. (College
Division)
Designer: Andrew P. Kner
Illustration: Old engravings on both
covers

*Theories of Education in
Early America 1655-1819*

EDITED BY WILSON SMITH

THE AMERICAN HERITAGE SERIES

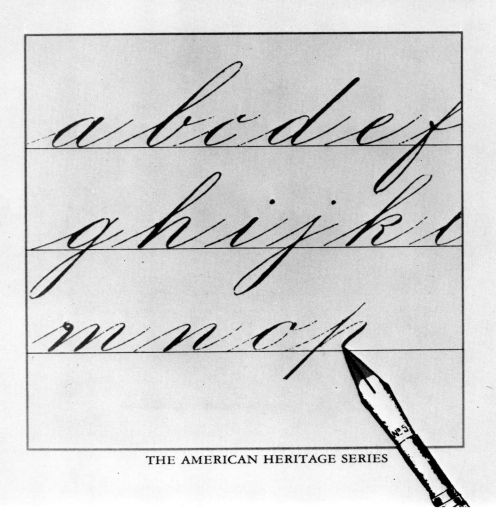

*American Writings on Popular Education:
the Nineteenth Century*

EDITED BY RUSH WELTER

THE AMERICAN HERITAGE SERIES

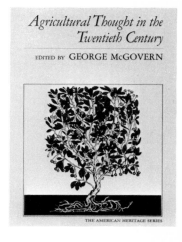

Agricultural Thought in the Twentieth Century

EDITED BY GEORGE McGOVERN

THE AMERICAN HERITAGE SERIES

American Military Thought

EDITED BY WALTER MILLIS

THE AMERICAN HERITAGE SERIES

Nonviolence in America

EDITED BY STAUGHTON LYND

THE AMERICAN HERITAGE SERIES

Other, earlier titles in series.

Rachmaninoff: Concerto No. 2 in C Minor

Graphic quality under rush deadlines is the norm at ABC Records. For this client, three in-house designers (including the art director) produce 440 album jackets a year. Though outside talent is used extensively, that still amounts to one jacket every three days per designer.

The graphic department's aim is to produce individual and relatively unique packaging designs starting with only the receipt of a title. Some streamlined techniques of necessity had to be developed to maintain quality output. Communication is informal between the graphics department and the producer, the artist, and his management. The client relies on the graphic department's judgment, efficiency, creativity and ability to solve problems without much intrusion. After a graphics department conference, the photography or illustration phase of the work proceeds without mockups or comps. Decisions are discussed by phone with interested parties; then the jacket goes into finish. Technical approval from the various departments is next sought, before the art goes to final film separation. At that point it is in the production department's hands, and is referred back to graphics only for quality control judgment.

The six album jackets shown here all evolved from that same quick process, with only one minor exception, noted later. The cover for the Rachmaninoff album was purchased from a student exhibit at Los Angeles' Art Center. The art director did not have a specific recording in mind when he bought it, but

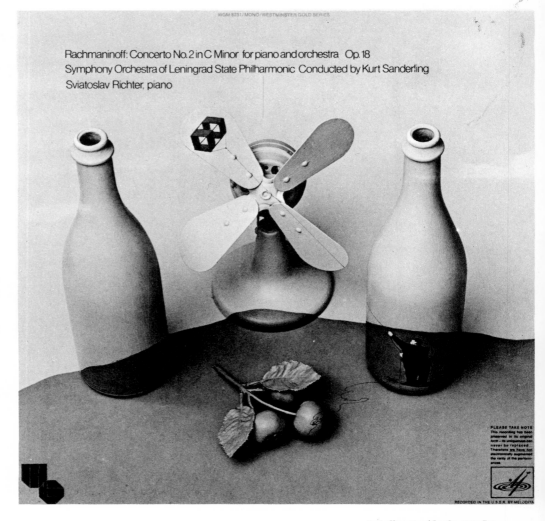

WGM 8231/MONO/WESTMINSTER GOLD SERIES

Rachmaninoff: Concerto No. 2 in C Minor for piano and orchestra Op. 18
Symphony Orchestra of Leningrad State Philharmonic Conducted by Kurt Sanderling
Sviatoslav Richter, piano

PLEASE TAKE NOTE

RECORDED IN THE U.S.S.R. BY MELODIYA

Art director/designer: Peter Whorf
Illustrator: Tim Bryant

knew he would be able to use it eventually. When the Rachmaninoff recording came along, that seemed to be the right opportunity.

The *Apple & Appleberry* title derives from the names of the two principals in the group. Apples and strawberries were literally packed together in a crate and photographed with a label bearing the album title name.

The jacket for *Locomotiv GT* posed a slight problem. Originally, the recording , made by what is probably the biggest rock group in the Communist countries , was scheduled to come out on very short notice. No artwork was provided. An all-night photography session was set up to take a hurried shot of a toy train. But the photo didn't capture the drive and energy of the group. Fortunately, the release date of the album was postponed, and there was enough time to commission a cover illustration that expressed the musical qualities of the recording.

The *Sonoma* album represents a group of "middle rock" musicians whose work conveys a kind of nostalgic "California" feeling. The illustrator executed the artwork in gold leafing on glass—his specialty—using acrylic and airbrush.

The jacket for *Fate in a Pleasant Mood* came about in much the same way as that for the Rachmaninoff work. The name itself was Sun Ra's idea, who likes to think of provocative, unusual titles. Reproduction rights to the cover painting were purchased from a portfolio which was brought into the client's office for review. The

Art director/designer: Peter Whorf
Illustrators: Ron Kriss, Joe Garnett
Photographer: Gene Brownell

artist lives and works in Taos, New Mexico; his work is strongly influenced by Indian images and symbols: deserts, serpents, plants, etc. The illustration fit the recording's title.

The title *Rufusized* was thought up by the recording group. The graphic department played around with two or three ideas, none of which really worked very effectively. While the cover was in its mid-concept stage there was a change of musicians in the group, and the decision was made to commission a photographer who works particularly well with rock groups to do the cover.

Art director/designer: Peter Whorf
Illustrator: Dave Willardson

DSX-50156

Art director: Peter Whorf
Designer/illustrator: Henry Beer

Sun Ra: Fate in a Pleasant Mood

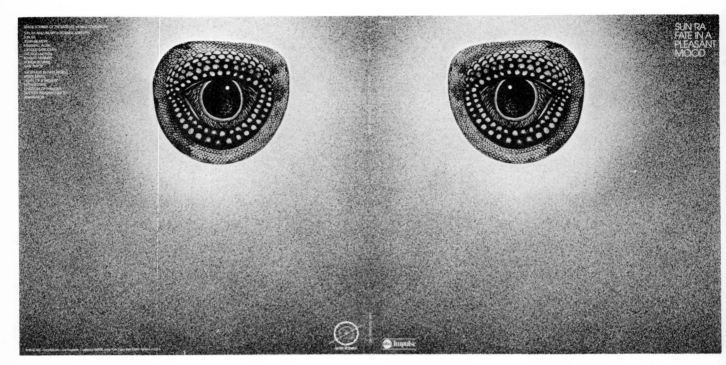

Art director: Peter Whorf
Designer: Tim Bryant
Illustrator: Bohdi Wind

Rufusized

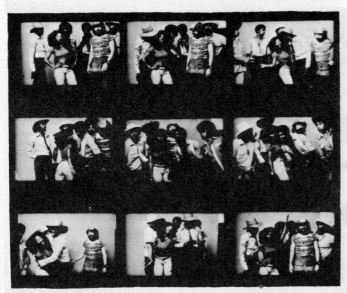

RUFUSIZED (INSTRUMENTAL) • ONCE YOU GET STARTED • STOP ON BY • PACK'D MY BAGS • YOUR SMILE • I'M A WOMAN (EVERYBODY NEEDS ONE) • SOMEBODY'S WATCHING YOU • PLEASE PARDON ME (YOU REMIND ME OF A FRIEND) • RIGHT IS RIGHT • HALF MOON

RUFUSIZED · RUFUS FEATURING CHAKA KHAN

Art director/designer: Earl Klasky
Photographer: Norman Seeff

Client: ABC Records, Inc.
Design firm: ABC Records Art
Dept., Los Angeles

The graphic idea for *The Rap* seemed so inevitable to the designer that there was never any question that it was the right solution. He worked on the placement of the type and the bars, and they fell into place with surprisingly natural ease. In the juxtaposition of type and photograph, note how the title itself appears to be behind bars.

Publisher: Atheneum
Art director: Harry Ford
Designer/photographer:
Lawrence Ratzkin

Kate Millett was enthusiastic about a cover she had seen at her publisher that was printed on silver paper, and from the very beginning of this project the concept of using silver paper with a fluorescent title was under consideration. There were no budgetary restrictions; the jacket was in fact very expensive compared to the average book cover. But the intent was to achieve so much individuality that the book would be instantly singled out in bookstores.

The first designs were rejected because the lettering on the title looked like skywriting. The author wanted a more direct approach. Once the sketch was accepted, only one modification was requested by the editor—the addition of hairline divisions between the letters of the title.

In the first proofs, the pink fluorescent silkscreened ink did not come out with a smooth, hard edge. Eventually the printer was able to maintain quality in the silkscreening, and the final results turned out to be far better than originally anticipated. What was most rewarding about the assignment was that the author and the editor wanted, and accepted, an unusual, provocative design. And the designer was able to create a jacket that was innovative in the manufacturing and printing aspects.

Publisher: Alfred A. Knopf (Random House, Inc.)
Art director/designer: Robert D. Scudellari
Lettering: Hal Fiedler

The Sun Book
Growing Wild

The cover art for both books is as appealing to grownups as it is to children, a sure test of graphic quality. The books comprise two of the titles in the publisher's reading series for children. They were entirely written, illustrated and designed by Marilyn Bass and Marvin Goldman, and were sold to the publisher from the manuscript in dummy form.

Both covers give the child strong clues as to what is going on inside the books, and they are integrally related to the contents. Book and cover have the same design plan, which is created not for style but to establish the proper mood for the subject.

The dandelion on the cover of *Growing Wild* is a favorite of the authors/designers. They wanted an illustration with a strong silhouette to create a "botanical yet free spirit." Other illustrations might have been more beautiful, but the dandelion was chosen because of its interesting silhouette. "We feel we have created a classical yet contemporary study of a flower for plant lovers of all ages."

Not surprisingly, the authors find that the freedom to create their own graphics is the most satisfying aspect of preparing the books for publication.

BY MARILYN BASS AND MARVIN GOLDMAN

Inside spreads.

Some places have very little sun.

The sun makes other places hot.

The sun dries grapes into raisins.

The sun dries clay pots.

Publisher: Macmillan Publishing Co., Inc.
Designers/illustrators: Marilyn Bass, Marvin Goldman

Inside spreads.

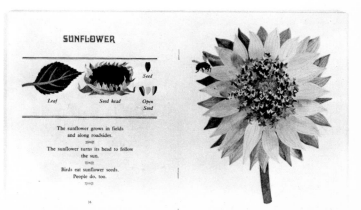

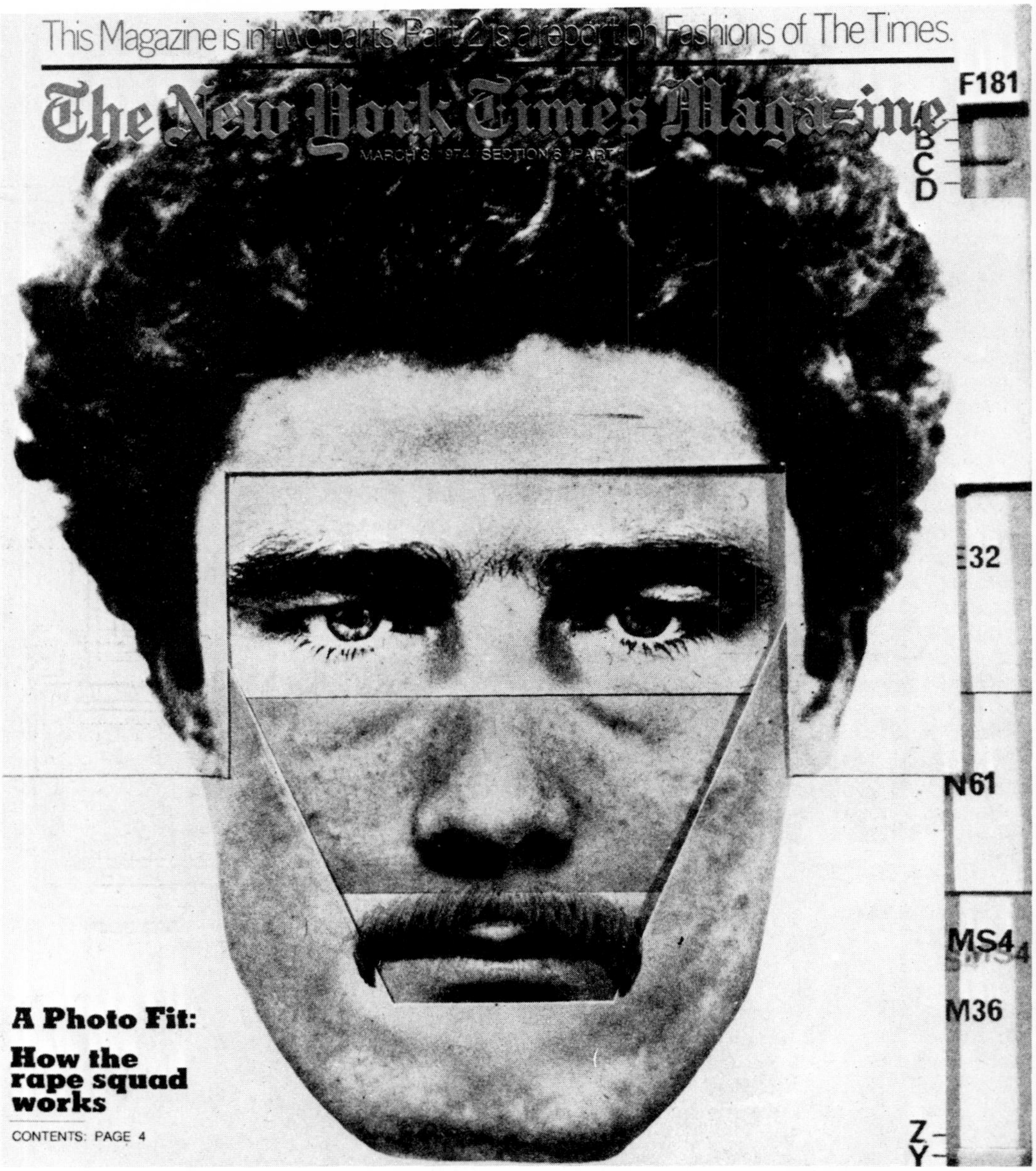

In recent years the New York Times has made great strides in graphically improving the various sections of both the daily and Sunday editions. The Op-Ed page, which has become one of the most popular features in the paper, uses some of the most sophisticated illustration appearing anywhere in the print media today. The Arts and Leisure Section of the Sunday edition has been completely redesigned, and other sections are expected to follow suit.

The covers of the Sunday Magazine have established themselves as the most creative part of this section. They are like an ongoing, open forum showing a diversity of graphic approaches from week to week. Partly because it is sold in the Sunday package, the Magazine is less fettered in its approach to cover art, color, typography, than most other publications that are found on the newsstand. It also has the advantage of a generous format—almost 11″ by 12¾″. Beyond trying to stimulate reader interest, the Magazine's covers are genuinely concerned with setting a proper context for the reader to approach the story. The collection of covers shown here is fairly representative of the wide range of visual approaches employed by art director Ruth Ansel— news pictures, high quality documentary photos, posters, typographic treatments, stylized illustration, etc.

A cover story on rape (March 3) posed a graphic challenge. Accurate photos cannot be used without invading an individual's privacy, whether it's a photo of a rapist or his victim. But because of the subject matter, a drawing

This Magazine is in two parts. Part 2 is a report on Fashions of The Times.

The New York Times Magazine

MARCH 3, 1974 SECTION 6 PART 1

F181
BCD
E32
N61
MS4₄
M36
Z
Y

A Photo Fit:
How the
rape squad
works

CONTENTS: PAGE 4

or painting was ruled out; it would have diminished the impact. In reviewing the possibilities, art director Ansel came across the idea of a police photo-kit—a collage of authentic images from real photographs, pieced together to comprise a "photo fit" which police use in criminal detection work. It provided a strong visual solution that left things open to

interpretation and avoided the invasion-of-privacy obstacle.

A bona fide breakthrough for the Sunday Magazine was its cover for a story about Penn Central (November 3). It marked the first time that the logo was reduced to fit inside the design. The overall design, including logo and blurb, were wholly integrated. To make these changes, Ansel had to get

approval from the editors. Initially there was great opposition to the idea, mainly because it had never been done before. But after lengthy discussion, they were persuaded.

No suggestions or editorial ideas were forthcoming from the author or the Sunday editor when the manuscript was presented to the art department.

The conventional approach—bad photos of packed trains in a yard—seemed stale. The train-logo poster was an appealing idea for its own sake, and also because the art director felt that it presented a unique opportunity for the artist involved. It was completed in five working days.

What proved most rewarding of all to Ansel was having a chance to change the cover shape and give it an uneven edge formed by the art. It was made to look like a shaped canvas rather than a normal square or rectangle. The unusual colors—off-shades of blue, blue-green, orange and yellow—helped make this one of the more visually arresting Magazine covers.

The cover story concerning an industrially-induced disease (issue of October 27) at first seemed difficult to illustrate. Photos of the outside of the factory, and photos of a doctor's office, were considered but found dull. Ansel then decided to use a photograph of a woman affected by the disease, and commissioned Bob Adelman to photograph her with her family at home in New Jersey. Because of the tone of the story, Ansel asked the editors to run it in sepia, not color. Initially they resisted, but she fought for the idea and finally won agreement. The most satisfying part of the assignment, according to Ansel, was working out the idea with the photographer and trusting him to take the right image: "It was a strong and moving visual—not a graphic solution as much as an emotionally revealing portrait that created the right mood for the article."

For an article on East-West

trade in a era of detente (issue of February 24), Ansel sought a poster-like effect on the cover. The first attempt showed the whole Pepsi-Cola bottle, but the results proved unsatisfying. By continually simplifying the design, she arrived at the solution selected, which focuses on the symbol with Pepsi-Cola written in Russian. The solution is an elegant one,

especially in its bright red and blue colors.

A wry, witty solution is the cover design made to look like a fight poster (September 8), which serves very effectively for a piece about Zaïre, Africa. The only alternatives were pictures of the country and its African leaders, but they were poor in quality, and not available in color. For Ruth Ansel the most

satisfying aspect of the assignment was working closely with the copywriter so that the design and message were coordinated and unified into a whole. There was one technical problem: getting the type to look realistically broken up, as it would in an actual poster. But that turned out not to be a problem, after all. Quips Ansel: "Our composing room only had

The New York Times Magazine
OCTOBER 27, 1974 / SECTION 6

Daughter of a hidden plague / CONTENTS: PAGE 13

The New York Times Magazine
FEBRUARY 24, 1974 SECTION 6

ПЕПСИ-КОЛА

The genie of East-West trade: Out of the bottle / CONTENTS: PAGE 9

The New York Times Magazine
SEPTEMBER 8, 1974 | SECTION 6

PRESIDENT MOBUTU PRESENTS
GEORGE
FOREMAN
★★ VS. ★★
MUHAMMAD ALI
IN
THE FIGHT TO PUT ZAÏRE ON THE MAP

Contents Page: 25

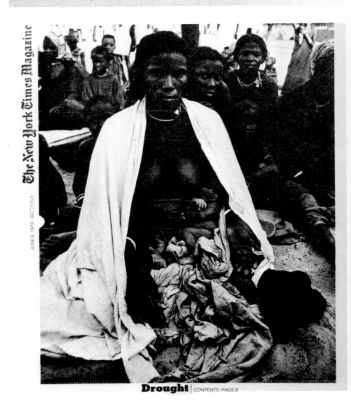

The New York Times Magazine
JUNE 9, 1974 SECTION 6

Drought | CONTENTS: PAGE 8

to set type as they normally do and all the imperfections I needed were there.''

There were no visuals provided at all with the manuscript of a story about drought and starvation (issue of June 9). The art director could have found a photo from the wire services, but that probably would have meant poor quality and low impact. Instead, she decided to search for a news photo from a distinguished photographer who had covered the African drought. Finding the original photos of Donald McCullin turned out to be the most satisfying aspect of the assignment. In fact, for Ansel this represents one of the best of the Sunday Magazine covers, because it is both a high quality photograph and a strong news picture.

The delightful Seymour Chwast chair cover (August 25) not only gives an unusual and most atypical look to the Magazine, but also provides a refreshingly satisfying design solution. This light touch works especially well as a counterpoint to the generally heavy going of the Magazine's articles. The alternative to this illustration for a piece on the role of the father in the family unit was a cover based on very sociological looking family scenes, which would have been far less imaginative and decidedly drab by comparison.

This Magazine is in two parts: Part 2 is a report on Fashions of The Times.

The New York Times Magazine

AUGUST 25, 1974 | SECTION 6 | PART 1

Whatever happened to Father? | CONTENTS: PAGE 2

Publisher: The New York Times Corp.
Art director/designer: Ruth Ansel
February 24, 1974:
Illustrator: Ruth Ansel
Copywriter: Jack Rosenthal
March 3, 1974:
Photographer: Lee Romero
Copywriter: Lewis Bergman
June 9, 1974:
Photographer: Donald McCullin
Copywriter: Lewis Bergman
August 25, 1974:
Illustrator: Seymour Chwast

September 8, 1974:
Collagist: Ruth Ansel
Copywriter: Jack Rosenthal
October 27, 1974:
Photographer: Bob Adelman
Copywriter: Jack Rosenthal
November 3, 1974:
Illustrator: Michael Doret
Copywriter: Jack Rosenthal

The Selected Poems
of Frank O'Hara

The artwork for the *Selected Poems* would probably have surfaced sooner or later, but it almost didn't appear on a book cover, for which it was originally designed, because of some unusual complications.

The late poet and art critic Frank O'Hara was closely associated with the so-called "New York school" artists, and his sister suggested to the publisher that Larry Rivers, a prominent member of the school, be asked to do the cover for the first major edition of the *Collected Poems.* No restrictions were placed on Rivers, though the sister's approval was needed in addition to the regular approvals. When she saw the finished cover she objected to the frontal nudity of her brother—though several of the poems explore homosexual themes—and the entire run had to be rejected.

A couple of years later the publisher planned an edition of the *Selected Poems,* and the sister was again approached about using the Rivers artwork. By then her attitude had changed, and she agreed.

This time around several technical problems presented themselves. The background color was very subtle; the artwork itself was a pencil drawing on top of a semi-transparent tissue. Since it was a "fine art" creation, art director Bob Scudellari felt that it was his (and the production head's) responsibility to supply a realistic camera-ready representation of Rivers' artwork to the printer. A further complicating factor was that the scale had changed; the original artwork had been designed for a much larger format. Thus it became necessary to retouch heavily, using a dye transfer to build the format that Rivers had intended.

There was concern about a lack of acceptance of the book in Bible Belt bookstores, but after thinking about the matter, the publishers agreed that the book wouldn't sell in such areas anyway. It was more important that it find its proper audience, which would be more than willing to accept the cover as it finally appeared.

Publisher: Alfred A. Knopf (Random House, Inc.)
Art director/designer: Robert D. Scudellari
Illustrator: Larry Rivers
Retouching: Ramer & Wolsk

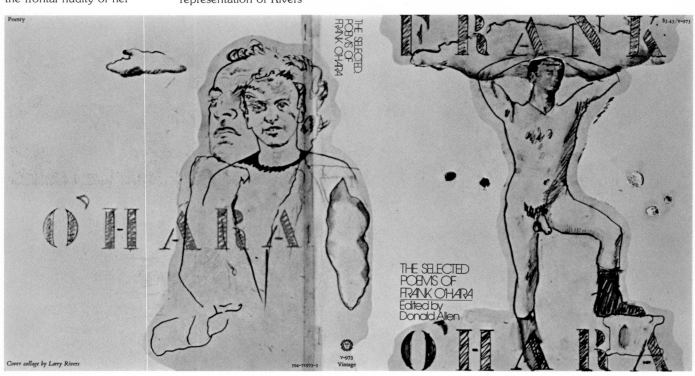

Cover collage by Larry Rivers

Lorraine Ellison

The original idea here was to have a color photograph of the artist on the cover. During the photography sessions, however, the art director found that black-and-white was actually more attractive than color, just because of skin tones. After the print was made, the four-color rainbow was put in to offset the black-and-white photo. The type was kept very unobtrusive, while remaining distinctly visible. The final result pleased everyone involved. The art director considers it "probably the nicest cover Lorraine Ellison has had, in my opinion."

Lorraine Ellison

Clients: Warner Bros. Records
Art director: Ed Thrasher
Designer: Chris Whorf
Photographer: Gary Gross

The Ikettes— (G)Old & New

The Ikettes are a group that have been around for many years and have gone through many changes in musical styles and singers. This was their first album of what is to be a collection of new recordings by the current Ikettes of hits recorded originally by the previous group, along with some new material.

The producer requested that a photo of the old Ikettes be included on the cover in addition to the current photo. The designer wanted to establish a new, contemporary image by presenting the Ikettes in a casual, funky, glamorous light.

The photo session was done at the client's photo studio. At one point, while the women were resting between set-ups, the art director suggested that they be photographed as they were, sitting on an old couch. That became the picture that was finally selected for the cover. The idea of using a combination of cartoon-like illustration along with the photograph was made in the art department. The design then evolved logically from the various elements.

For designer Lloyd Ziff, the most interesting aspect of the result was the humor, which was readily accepted by the recording group and the client.

Client: United Artists Records
Art director: Mike Salisbury
Design firm: United Artists Art Dept., Los Angeles
Designer: Lloyd Ziff
Illustrator: Mick Haggerty
Photographer: Fred Valentine

Succotash

The design of the Succotash album illustrates the old "less is more" adage. Here, least is most. There were no design restrictions, except that the names of the players had to be featured along with the title in the upper half of the album for prominent display in the record rack.

The recording features two prominent jazz artists, and the title derives its name from the dish, succotash, consisting of two ingredients—lima beans and corn. This inspired art director/designer/photographer Mike Salisbury's recipe: "Take one bean, one kernel, place on restaurant plate, photograph with Kodachrome in bright sunlight, add a dash of retouching to clean up the plate, garnish with City Bold type lightly letter-spaced, print on a four-color webb, and finish off with a double varnish for that just-cooked look."

Client: United Artists Records
Design firm: United Artists Art Dept., Los Angeles
**Art director/designer/
photographer:** Mike Salisbury

German Expressionism inspired the cover design for this novel about the harrowing reality of war for a child. (The artists of that movement were persecuted and destroyed by the Nazis.) The original sketch used a tighter and heavier woodcut lettering style for the title, in keeping with Expressionist practice. The editor objected on the grounds that it was hard to read, and recommended a set typeface. The issue was resolved with a small compromise. The lettering was somewhat refined, but its strength and unity were retained. The final result came very close to the original design. For the artist, the most satisfying aspect was being able to develop a total environment on paper, without being forced into a more common, safe solution.

Publisher: Viking Press
Art director: Kate Westray
Designer/illustrator: Barbara Bascove

Hollywood and LeVine

LeVine is a crack New York private eye who goes out to Los Angeles on an assignment involving a screenwriter's wife accused of Communist affiliations. Richard M. Nixon, then a young congressman from California, figures in the story as the chief Red-baiter, out to make a national reputation for himself. This comic detective novel by the author of *Blazing Saddles* is set in the late forties and uses all the film industry and L.A. backdrops. The cast of characters includes Bogart and Bacall and other Hollywood notables.

The cover set out to capture the feeling of the book. Cliché is deliberately used to recreate the look of the period, which is interpreted through a broad and flat illustration style. The sultry figures set against the studio backlots, and the title painted in vintage forties' script, serve to provide exactly the right tone for the book.

Publisher: Holt, Rinehart and Winston
Art director: Robert Reed
Designers: Robert Reed, Stanislaw Zagorski
Illustrator: Stanislaw Zagorski

Columbia Records is involved in so many different categories of music—classical, pop, rock, jazz—that no single approach or cover style could encompass them all. Each record is therefore approached as a new problem with its own requirements. The basic idea is to package the album to fit the music. There are areas, however, where the requirements are similar enough—as in recordings of Beethoven quartets or Billie Holiday albums—that a consistent cover style is called for.

On the other hand, there seems to be a trend toward applying more popular standards to classical record covers, and vice versa. As the art director puts it, ''Lines are getting blurred.'' Everyone on the design staff is involved in all kinds of cover design. No one specializes in classical music, or pop.

The jackets shown here reflect the diversity of approaches. The *Charles Ives* cover draws upon photographs, illustrations and other visual materials in the CBS Ives collection—the largest such body of materials anywhere. Illustrator Dick Hess used those resources to create a cover teeming with references to a kind of golden-age Americana that was part of Ives' environment. It is particularly appropriate here because Ives' music is a curious blend of avant-gardism and vernacular American tunes—atonalism mixed with ''Pop Goes the Weasel,'' at times. The busyness of the cover is meant to reflect the fullness of the record's contents.

Art director: John Berg (New York office)
Designer: Henrietta Condak
Illustrator: Richard Hess

Santana's Greatest Hits

The *Santana* album design originated from a promotion poster that happened to be hanging in the CBS offices when the record came along. It seemed to fit Santana's personality to perfection: the artist himself is very black, and peace-oriented. It also had musical rightness: his music reflects the sound of a rhythm band. The powerful photograph plays on black-and-white symbolism, and on peace symbolism traditionally associated with the dove.

The *Miles Davis* cover is a portrait of the artist, created by taking a photograph and putting it through the laboratory to enhance the chiaroscuro effect. It is printed in brown. The solution was not only graphically sound, giving a strong, clean cover; it also served to overcome a serious rush deadline problem.

The *Loggins and Messina* album was more problematic than the others, but it proves that good covers can result even after budget restrictions and client demands impose changes and ''compromises.'' The assignment was to create a package for a two-record album of live performances. In addition to attracting record store sales, the design had to lend itself to blow-ups and posters utilizing the album package.

One of the artists, Jim Messina, suggested photographing the band either on a real stage or on a stagecoach. The art director rejected both approaches, feeling that neither was strong enough to come across. ''Live photographs of groups on covers are done too much for live albums,'' he explains.

Art director/designer: John Berg (New York office)
Photographer: Joel Baldwin

Miles Davis: Get Up with It

The ticket-like concept was developed by the art director, but there were changes from the original sketch. For one thing, the ticket idea was enlarged. And the musicians felt strongly that their picture should appear on the cover. The art director tried to convince them that no picture should be printed, and that a black line drawing might be used instead. They ended with a compromise: a small inset oval photograph of the two principal musicians on front and back covers (the two covers are identical, separated by perforation-like dots to suggest a ticket roll), and more photos of the band on the inside of the album.

The positive part of the experience, according to the art director, was "to arrive at a satisfying agreement between Jim Messina and myself and walk away with a successful package."

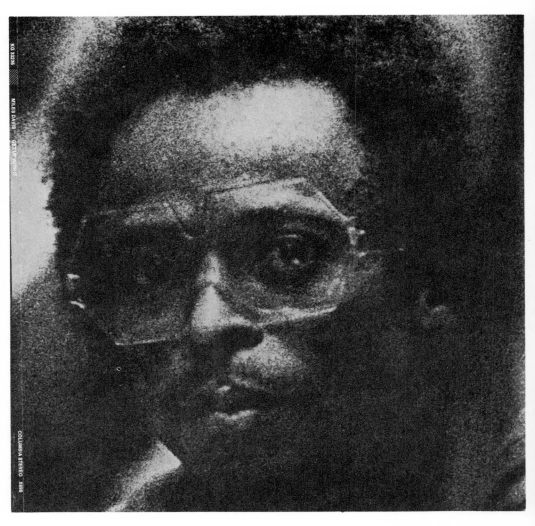

Art director: John Berg (New York office)
Designers: Teresa Alfieri
Photographer: Giuseppe Pino

Art director: Ron Coro (Hollywood office)
Designers: John and Barbara Casado
Illustrator: Tyler Thorton
Copywriter: Jack Breschard, Ellen Wolff

Client: Columbia Records
Design firm: CBS Records Art Dept., New York and Hollywood

Cover art on most sex magazines is largely restricted to breasts and buttocks (or "tits-and-ass" in the usual parlance). But these magazines are usually male-oriented. What distinguishes Viva is that it is directed toward women. It tries to be more than a soft-core romp, and publishes feminine-interest stories as well as nude pictures. The cover approach, therefore, tends to be more subtle than that of its competitors, emphasizing the sensuous and erotic over the blatantly obvious.

Cover ideas originate with the art director and are reviewed by the publisher. Often, a lot of back-and-forth discussion takes place before a cover is finally selected. When a choice is made, it will probably be feminine and appealing—like the April and June issues shown here. Both covers rely on good photography and a tasteful, esthetic handling of colors, typography and logo for their effect.

THE INTERNATIONAL MAGAZINE FOR WOMEN   APRIL   74 $1.00

VIVA

THE SENSUALIST·SANTANA & McLAUGHLIN:MORE SOUL THAN MIND
MAKING LOVE WITH THE KIDS AROUND·DRUG CHIC:NEW HIGH IN DOWNERS
PLUS ALL KINDS OF BEAUTIFUL PEOPLE IN THE NUDE

Publisher: Penthouse/Viva
International
Art director: Ahmad Sadiq
Designers: Frank Devino, Hector
Marrero
Photographers: Stan Shaffer
(April), Art Kane (June)

Babe Ruth and the American Dream

A spate of books on the same subject had recently been published when this book was coming out. Most of them idolized the Babe, neglecting the human, erring side of his nature. But this cover had to portray the complete man, in a format suitable to all mass-market channels of distribution, including drugstores and supermarkets.

Provided with manuscript, photos, fact sheet and author access, the illustrator developed a highly detailed montage that incorporated plenty of visual material about Ruth's life: photos, news clippings, filmstrips. Though the paperback publisher had initiated this project and commissioned the design—a reversal over the usual procedure—the hardcover publisher used the same art for its edition.

Publisher: Ballantine Books
Art director: Ian Summers
Designer: Carl Berkowitz
Illustrator: Cliff Condak
Copywriter: David Glazier

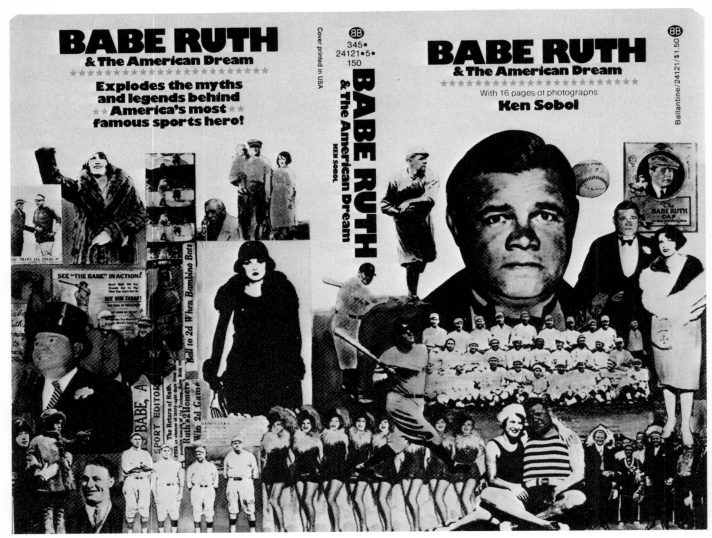

The budget for this book about an urban teen-age gang in the Bronx during the early '60s pre-Beatle days didn't permit original photography, though it did allow full-color process. The designers had to research stock photographs and adjust their ideas to fit what was available. When they did find the photo, they encountered a problem with press separation: seven overlays were required to achieve the right results.

Only one change was made during the design phase. The title was originally in a hand-lettered graffiti style. The editor requested that the type be changed to a standard photo-lettering.

The result is a cover that captures the period of the book's subject with striking recognition.

Publisher: Houghton Mifflin
Art director: Louise Noble
Designers: Karen Batten, Elliot Kreloff
Photographer: Magnum

Humor, satire, parody, pun are the stuff of the National Lampoon, and every cover becomes a visual joke summarizing clues to the magazine's contents. A readily understandable image with an immediately recognizable point has to be created for newsstand impact.

The idea for the June 1974 issue—a girl holding a cornucopia overflowing with junk food—was conceived by the copywriter. The ultimate solution, however, evolved through several additional steps. A wooden crate was built, the magazine's logo was silk-screened on it, and the artwork was used like a food packaging label. The entire ensemble was then photographed. An important modification to the sketch was to heighten the contrast between the artificial food growing in the landscape background and the healthy-looking sunshine girl. The joke absolutely depended on people perceiving the discrepancy.

The *1964 High School Yearbook Parody* is probably the best-selling special project in the magazine's history. The cover joke is based on a mixture of humorous nostalgia for the '60s and the sexual fantasies of adolescence. The element of surprise created effective newsstand appeal, and the cover concept related appropriately to the editorial content.

The cover concept, which was originally planned for the cheerleader's page inside the magazine, was based on a common high school fantasy. It was the magazine's board chairman, Matty Simmons, who

suggested it for the cover. The editors agreed, but realized that it was crucial that the photograph be believable. If it came off as a manipulated studio shot or a stripped-in retouch job, the whole effect would be lost. And in costumes, clothing and hair styles, it had to say "1964."

This posed several problems. One was finding a school whose students and administration would allow Lampoon to use them as the cast, which effectively ruled out public schools. The documentary approach brought up problems with nudity, because students were not of legal age and parental reaction had to be considered. Eventually these hurdles were overcome. A small inner-city private school was found whose administration was willing to let the students pose for the cast. And the nude-bottomed model was not technically nude: she was shot wearing sheer, flesh-colored panties. The photograph was then retouched.

The budget for the cover was adequate, but it was almost twice as high (over $1000) as the usual Lampoon cover budget. The popularity of the finished product made the extra expense well worthwhile, given the enormously successful sales the publication enjoyed.

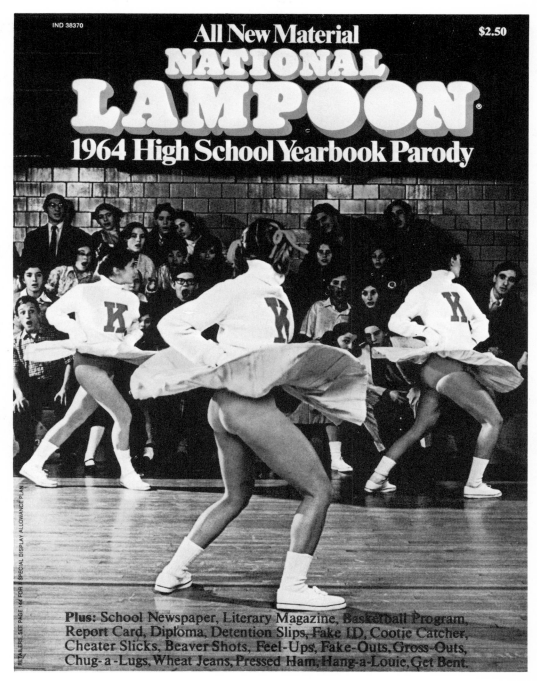

IND 38370

All New Material
NATIONAL LAMPOON
1964 High School Yearbook Parody

$2.50

RETAILERS, SEE PAGE 144 FOR A SPECIAL DISPLAY ALLOWANCE PLAN

Plus: School Newspaper, Literary Magazine, Basketball Program, Report Card, Diploma, Detention Slips, Fake I.D., Cootie Catcher, Cheater Slicks, Beaver Shots, Feel-Ups, Fake-Outs, Gross-Outs, Chug-a-Lugs, Wheat Jeans, Pressed Ham, Hang-a-Louie, Get Bent.

Food Issue:
Publisher: 21st Century Communications, Inc.
Design firm: Pellegrini, Kaestle & Gross, Inc., New York
Art director/designer: Michael Gross
Illustrator: Melinda Bordelon
Photographer: R.G. Harris
Copywriter: Tony Hendra
High School Yearbook:
Publisher: 21st Century Communications, Inc.
Design firm: National Lampoon Art Department
Art director/designer: David Kaestle

Photographer: Vince Aiosa
Stylist: Laura Singer
Copywriters: P.J. O'Rourke, Douglas Kenney

The cover of this biography is a collage made up of four different woodcut illustrations found in an old Islamic manuscript. All of the figures and elements are essentially symbolic and relate to episodes in Mohammed's life.

The illustrator sought a primitive Byzantine look, which comes through in the mosaic-like intensity of the colors.

Publisher: Vintage Books (Random House, Inc.)
Art director/designer: Judith Loeser
Illustrator: Elias Dominguez

MAXIME RODINSON
MOHAMMED

$3.95/V-67

Mary Wollstonecraft Shelley's gothic tale of terror inspired this science-fiction novel. A quality fiction look was required on the cover. Since Frankenstein had pieced together his nameless monster from flesh and bones from the charnel house, a straightforward cover treatment was indicated. An earlier sketch was rejected for being too complicated, and in the present version a background figure was eliminated. The focus was entirely on what Frankenstein's stitched-together creation looked like.

Publisher: Random House, Inc.
Art director: Robert D. Scudellari
Designer/illustrator: Paul Bacon

Giacometti sculptures are used for Kafka titles in the Vintage paperback series (see below). This cover is the exception, because nothing in Giacometti's work visually suggests the symbolic quality of that unattainable place that Land Surveyor K. eternally but hopelessly seeks to reach.

The art director was familiar with Magritte's painting (titled "The Castle of the Pyramids"), and had always wanted to use it on a cover. Its symbolic character was far more fitting for the Kafka work than anything in Giacometti, and it lent itself to effective positioning for a strong poster for the book.

Another title in Kafka series.

Publisher: Vintage Books (Random House, Inc.)
Art director/designer: Robert D. Scudellari
Illustrator: René Magritte

THE CASTLE
FRANZ KAFKA

$2.45   V-991   394-71991-3

With an Homage by Thomas Mann   Definitive Edition

Art director Judith Loeser asked
the illustrator, Thomas Upshur,
to provide a head for the cover,
but the rest is his concept. Arthur
Koestler's account of a
sensational and bitter scientific
feud concerning experiments in
evolution suggested the
eerie-looking head of the toad
emerging from a test tube-like
container. The art director
specified Chwast Blimp as the
typeface, filled it with horizontal
lines to give a shaded effect.

Publisher: Vintage Books (Randon
House, Inc.)
Art director/designer: Judith
Loeser
Illustrator: Thomas Upshur

$1.65/V-823

ARTHUR
KOESTLER
THE CASE OF THE
MIDWIFE
TOAD

"Reads like a thriller"—*Esquire*

In addition to various educational publications, Scholastic Magazines publishes entertainment magazines for pre-teen-agers which are ordered through schools. The main criterion is that they be fun to look at and appealing to elementary-age children. The cover of Dynamite magazine features a story on Snoopy, the redoubtable character in "Peanuts." The art director was provided only with line art and headline. His task was to give some interest to simple black-and-white line art by surrounding Snoopy with a colored background and putting the headline in skywriting. The logo is multi-colored—yellow, orange, purple, blue.

The untitled cover was created for an experimental magazine, and it had to be produced as inexpensively as possible. Because the magazine was new, there were no established design requirements, apart from the fact that the cover had to please the art director, editor and audience. After considering many alternatives, the art director eventually worked out a photo collage using elements from inside the issue, a solution which appealed because it was visually exciting and fun to work on.

Dynamite:
Publisher: Scholastic Magazines, Inc.
Art director: Greg Wozney
Design firm: Wozney and Lucik Design, New York
Designers: Greg Wozney, Richard Lucik
Illustrators: Charles Schultz, Phil Stagter
Copywriter: Jane Stine
Untitled:
Publisher: Scholastic Magazine, Inc.
Art director/designer: Skip Sorvino
Illustrators: Skip Sorvino, Donald Brautigam
Copywriter: Mel Cebulash

The Gunfighters

Each of the Time-Life Books series has its own distinctive look that reflects the mood and editorial concept of the project. The books are initially sold by direct mail.

When the concept for the Old West series was established, the art director and design staff became involved in creating a graphic solution which included all phases of book design. The tooled leather look of an old Western saddle was developed as an appropriate and unusual design approach for books on the Old West, and it was readily accepted by the publisher.

The covers are made of Lexotone 10-pt. kid finish in a special brown (from Holliston Mills). On a padded stock, they are blind stamped, gold stamped and hand-rubbed to give an antique look. An appropriate four-color print is tipped on to the cover of each book in the series. For this title, E.C. Ward's painting of a Western sheriff was used. The books and covers are printed by Kingsport Press in Kingsport, Tennessee.

Publisher: Time-Life Books
Art director: Sheldon Cotler
Designer: Albert Sherman
Illustrator: Nicholas Fasciano

Other, earlier titles in Old West series: The Indians, The Forty-Niners, The Expressman.

The cover is the only place in every issue of Art Direction where original art can be published. Except for occasional tie-ins when there are issues about illustration or photography, covers are totally independent of the contents. The art director looks for ''in'' covers—the most beautiful or unusual original art being done by commercial artists who have a chance to present themselves as they want, without commercial restrictions. Since the magazine is sold by subscription and in art supply stores, newsstand considerations are minimal. The only information provided the artist is a deadline.

The June 1974 cover was selected from among three submitted by Don Weller as being the most unusual. The artist describes it as ''spirited, whimsical, and slightly crazed, but open-ended. You can interpret it in various ways. To me it is an abstraction symbolizing the idea process.''

Publisher: Art Direction
Art director: Stanley Steller
Designer/illustrator: Don Weller

art direction

the magazine of visual communication   june 1974 $1.25

The Force is the name that art director Ed Thrasher gave to stars and performers who record for Warner Brothers in the Burbank, California, studio. He conceived and executed the idea of a two-record promotional sampler album as part of a total campaign for Warner. It included not only the album cover but also a "Force" poster, four-color trade ads, four-color T-shirts, leather wallets designed like real policemen's wallets, and cast gold badges, which are given to salesmen and promotion people.

The record set is ordered by direct mail only. For Thrasher, the most satisfying aspect of the design is that it worked as a total unit with all the elements coming together for a solid, thorough campaign.

Client: Warner Bros. Records
Art director: Ed Thrasher
Design firm: Warner Bros. Art Dept., Burbank, CA
Designer/copywriter: Ed Thrasher
Illustrator: Peter Palombi

The Fall

All of the Camus titles in the Vintage paperback series to date have used photography on the cover (see below). One previous sketch for *The Fall* using a Magritte sculpture was rejected as being "too impersonal." A subject that would "humanize" the cover was felt to be necessary.

Art director Bob Scudellari discovered this photograph in a magazine. He contacted the photographer, who readily agreed to let him use it and was pleased that it would appear on the cover of a major literary work.

The face in the photograph was in black-and-white, and the feather covering the eye lacked intensity. A dye transfer was necessary to heighten coloration of the face and intensity of the feather.

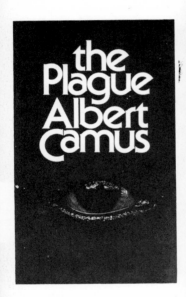

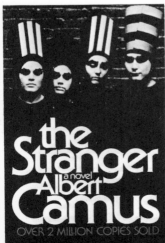

Other titles in Camus series.

Publisher: Vintage Books (Random House, Inc.)
Art director/designer: Robert D. Scudellari
Photographer: Paul Paree

On its covers Ms. uses straight photography (the kind of close-ups of faces or of joltingly real situations that pop out of the page at you), "reworked" photography, and illustrations. Of the two examples shown here, one tends to be more dynamic, the other more evocative, but each is strong and appealing in its own way. They are also completely representative of the forthright, interesting and informative editorial approach that the magazine takes.

For a cover story about women in the movies and how their image has changed in the last 40 years, the art director selected three movie stars (Greta Garbo, Joan Crawford, Doris Day) to symbolize three different periods of filmmaking. The sketch was worked out in the magazine's offices one quick afternoon with the illustrator, who then returned to Paris where she completed the illustration and sent it in by mail two weeks later. The fan-shaped composition of the three heads, and the airbrush technique, lend the painting what the art director calls "a sort of modern nostalgia feeling." It was the fourth best-selling cover in the magazine's history.

Capturing women in action sports (of a kind not traditionally associated with women) was the object of the second cover. Several color photos were considered, but this one, originally in black-and-white, was chosen for its impact. The photograph was tinted, but there was still too much black road in the background. More brightness and contrast were needed. The solution was to have the engraver strip-in a flat

area of process yellow background. This, along with the dynamic obliqueness of bikers banking a curve, gives it a strikingly attractive poster quality.

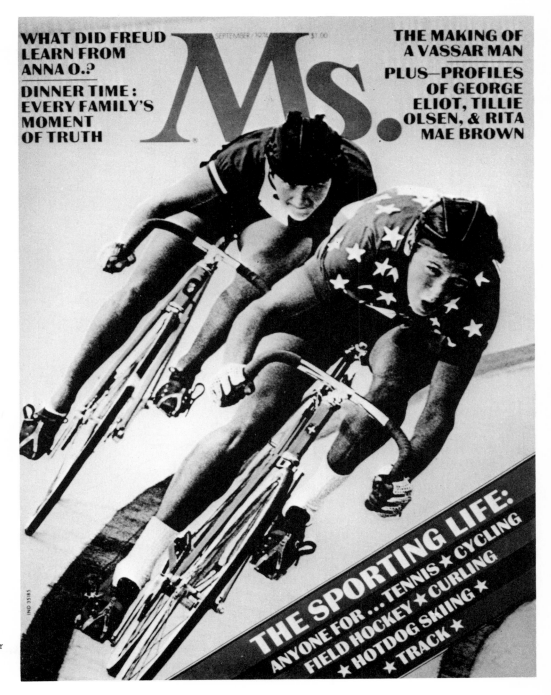

WHAT DID FREUD LEARN FROM ANNA O.?

DINNER TIME: EVERY FAMILY'S MOMENT OF TRUTH

SEPTEMBER / 1974 $1.00

Ms.

THE MAKING OF A VASSAR MAN

PLUS—PROFILES OF GEORGE ELIOT, TILLIE OLSEN, & RITA MAE BROWN

IND 35185

THE SPORTING LIFE:
ANYONE FOR ... TENNIS ★ CYCLING ★ FIELD HOCKEY ★ CURLING ★ ★ HOTDOG SKIING ★ ★ TRACK ★

Publisher: Ms.
Art director/designer: Bea Feitler
Illustrator: Liz Bijl ("Movies")
Photographer: Robert F. George ("Sporting Life")

The hyacinth was a favorite flower of the Romantics, associated with death, mourning, sadness, compassion. This cover illustration was immediately accepted from a rough tissue sketch. The beautifully-executed painting gives a strong, almost surreal visual solution, with the veins of the sensitive writer's hand nourishing the plant. The designer kept the type simple and clean, not to interfere with the sensitivity of the painting.

Publisher: New American Library
Art director: James Plumeri
Designer: Anthony Russo
Illustrator: Mark English
Copywriter: Ruth Haberstroh

Because this is a collection of science-fiction stories by several writers, illustrator Peter Lloyd suggested a generalized symbol of a head-like figure that could equally well represent any or all of the stories in the book. This is appropriate in the case of collected writings where no individual's work should be featured above another's. The "dated" airbrush technique is peculiarly suited to the subject matter; it smacks of the thirties, of course, but thirties' artists were always producing streamlined, futuristic images that looked just like this.

SIGNET·451-Y6113·$1.25

EDITED BY
ROBERT SILVERBERG
NEW DIMENSIONS
IV

FEATURING:
R. A. LAFFERTY
TERRY CARR
BARRY N. MALZBERG
RICHARD A. LUPOFF

DAVID R. BUNCH
GARDNER R. DOZOIS
LAURENCE M. JANIFER
FELIX C. GOTSCHALK
ROGER ELWOOD

Publisher: New American Library
Art director: James Plumeri
Designer: Anthony Russo
Illustrator: Peter Lloyd
Copywriter: Ruth Haberstroh

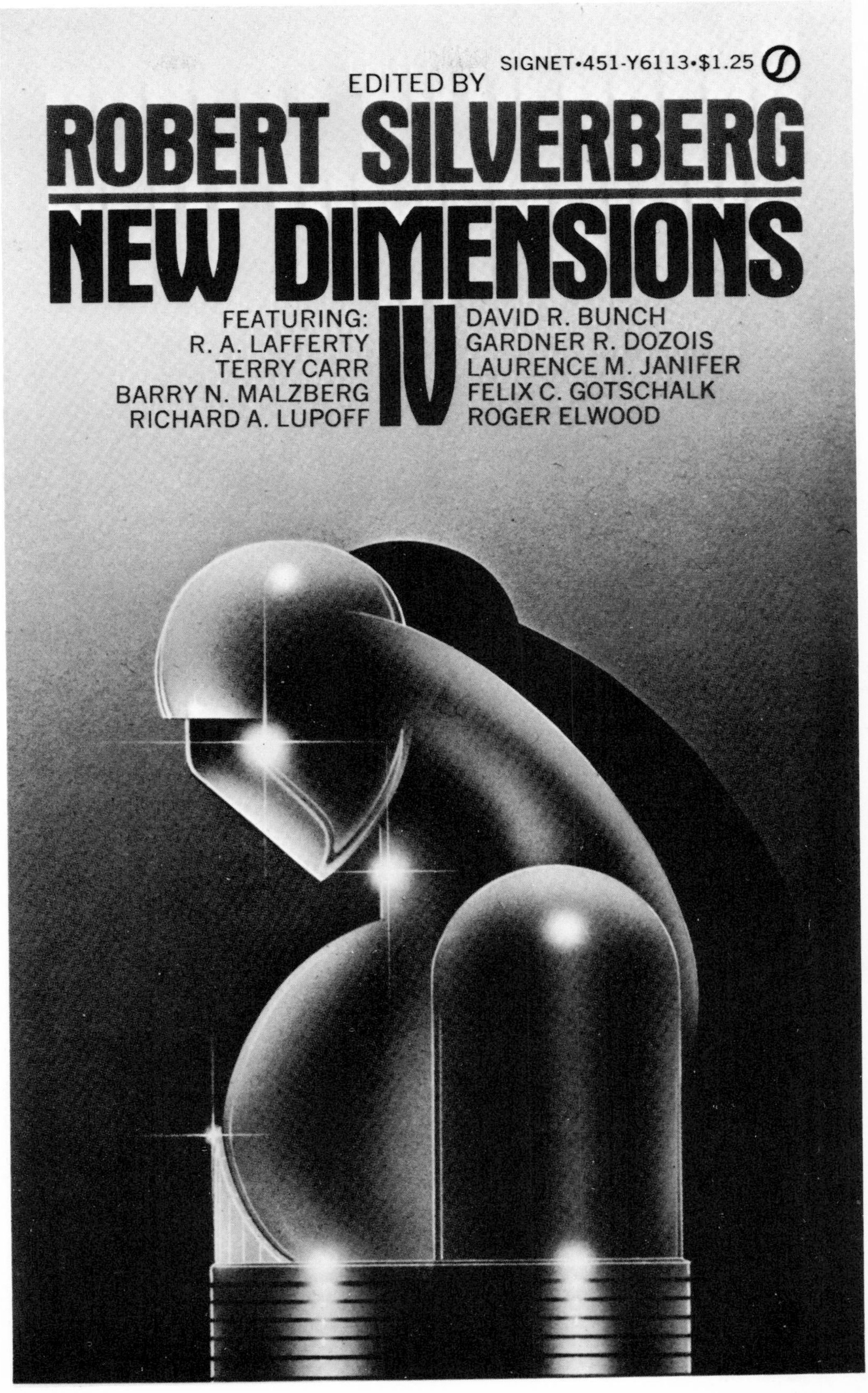

Few trade magazines seem to sustain a fresh approach with stylistic consistency from issue to issue. This one does, in large part because the designer has the freedom to pursue design development. The magazine is mailed to subscribers in a sealed envelope, and so there is no need for large, punchy (i.e., newsstand-style) headlines. Printing is limited to three colors, one of which must always be black and the second of which must always be process red, and so a great deal of care is taken to achieve variety and effectiveness through the use of screens.

The problem presented by the March issue was to portray shop towels, which are nothing more than rags cut to a uniform size. They were shown being used on printing press rollers, because printers' towels cause the greatest problems in industrial laundering. The third color here was process yellow. ("The color of the bottom towel surprised us by appearing greener than we had expected," says designer Jack Lefkowitz.)

The April issue featured an article on a young girl working as a route driver for a uniform rental company. The design objective was to take a masculine environment and introduce a feminine symbol into it. There were some black-and-white photographs of the girl at the wheel of her truck, but they were rejected along with any attempt to illustrate from them. A yellow rose placed on the steering wheel answered the need in a fresh, simple and direct way.

Industrial
Launderer
March
1974

Publisher: Institute of Industrial
Launderers
Art director: Jack Lefkowitz
Design firm: Jack Lefkowitz, Inc.,
Washington, D.C.
Designers/illustrators: Jack and
Pam Lefkowitz

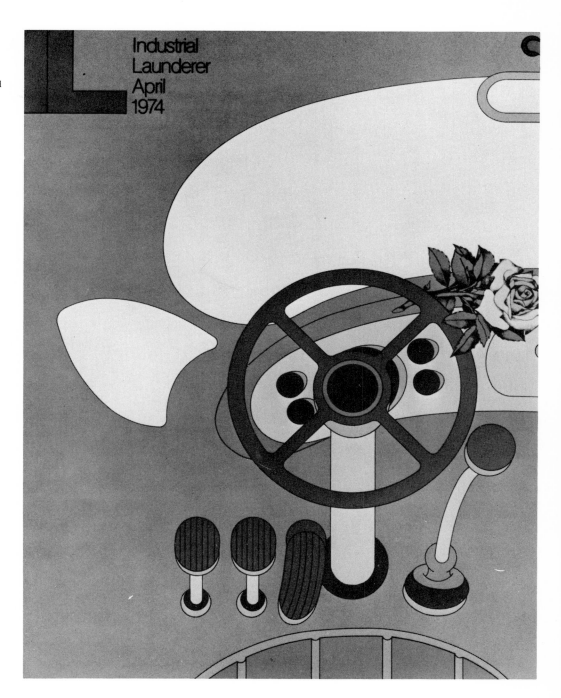

Industrial
Launderer
April
1974

This cover created something of a sensation at its publisher. When the first tight sketch was turned in, everyone, including people who normally don't pay much attention to things like covers, responded with enthusiasm. On the basis of the cover, the publisher decided to turn the book into a whole series. Work is already underway on the next title, *Indians of the Plains.*

The book is distributed to school-age children in the fourth through seventh grades via schools and public libraries. Because bookstore sales are not a factor, the illustrator/designer was free to avoid the hard-sell and develop an individual approach. This was done by emphasizing the type design and avoiding any trace of cliché which so often mars graphic work relating to Indian themes.

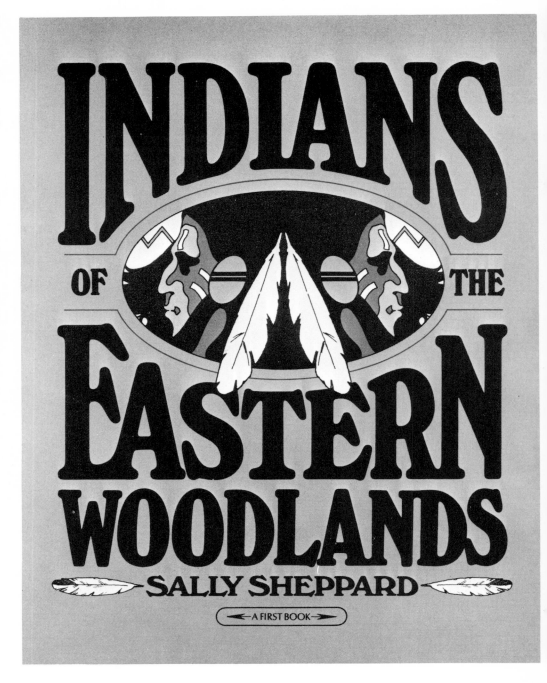

Publisher: Franklin Watts, Inc.
Art director: Judie Mills
Designer/illustrator: Paul Gamarello

Contract Bridge Complete

The back of a playing card inspired the cover design of this book. It was adapted to make a strong, effective book jacket. The coloring (red, yellow, blue) was made as bright and posterish as possible. The design successfully fulfills the two basic criteria that all book covers—in designer Bea Feitler's eyes—should possess: a strong basis in the book's content, and an irresistibility so compelling that the consumer says: "I must buy that book."

Publisher: Simon & Schuster
Art director: Frank Metz
Designer: Bea Feitler

Both titles on this spread are published in the Dell Yearling Book series for young readers. The graphic department attempted, as it does with all covers, to set them apart from the competitors by giving them an attractive and unique look.

Killer of Death strives for a distinctively different approach to a Western. The art director and illustrator worked together to develop a sketch that would permit placement of the type in the middle of the cover. The result came out exactly as planned.

For *The Case of the Elevator Duck*—a whodunit for six-to-nine-year-olds—a light and humorous illustration that avoided a cartoonish look seemed to be the right approach. The scene in the book where boy meets duck provided the illustration subject. Typeface that was light, informal and bouncy was sought for the title. Cooper Outline was selected.

A DELL YEARLING BOOK 1.25

An ancient way of life comes to a violent end

KILLER OF DEATH
Betty Baker

The Case of the
Elevator Duck

Publisher: Dell Publishing
Art director: Bruce Hall
Killer of Death:
Designer: Bruce Hall
Illustrator: Jack Andewwlt
Elevator Duck:
Designers: Bruce Hall, P. Williamson
Illustrator: Jo-Anne Scribner
Copywriter: Rich Samuelson

A DELL YEARLING BOOK   75c

A boy detective takes on an unusual case

THE CASE OF THE ELEVATOR DUCK

Polly Berrien Berends

In 1974, Robert Moses was the subject of a critical and widely-discussed book, the Pulitzer Prize-winning *The Power Broker,* by former Newsday reporter Anthony Caro. Over a 50-year career this most powerful of New York commissioners had almost single-handedly shaped the development pattern of Long Island.

The series of excerpts from the book published by Newsday's "Magazine for Long Island" suggested to designer/illustrator Gary Viskupic (who was involved from the beginning) the idea of taking the initial color cover assignment one step further and proposing a tie-in with an inside illustration. Specifically, says Viskupic, "the idea was to depict Mr. Moses, of World's Fair and highway, park, and housing planning fame (infamy?) in Biblical garb as that other Moses, parting the sea to Long Island and bringing all his ideas ('commandments') for highways, parks, etc. Then, as one turned into the magazine to the feature story, a full-page illustration was used. It depicted Moses after his crossing to Long Island as the 'power broker,' an emperor/tyrant implanted as a self-erected (though flawed) monument surrounded by his accomplishments."

Since the secondary drawing was not originally intended to be full page, which art director Cliff Gardiner thought necessary to tie in with the concept, some juggling had to be done to get space for the full-page illustration.

Both color cover and black-and-white inside illustration were originally allotted three weeks for completion, but the color deadline suddenly was shortened at the last minute to two weeks instead of three. Gardiner recalls working right up to deadline, reworking and splicing the tablets, trying to find a way to fit the map of Long Island onto them.

Under the heading "Minor Disaster Averted," Viskupic reports the following:

"Originally, the cover design was intended to have a diagonal band of type in the upper right-hand corner calling attention to a secondary story on interior design. This is why the figure is so situated, with the expanse of sky on the right. Lightning bolts were to be incorporated in this space, but it was felt they would muddle up the type overlay. It turned out, however, that everyone violently objected to the wordy type diagonal, and it was dropped—thanks, primarily, to the protestations of photo editor Harvey Weber."

Publisher: Newsday
Art director: Cliff Gardiner
Designer/illustrator: Gary Viskupic
Copywriter: Phillippe Sanborne

Drawing from inside magazine.

The original proposal for this cover called for a typographic treatment. The idea was rejected, however, because it was felt that more visual interest was needed for a muckraking exposé of corporate giantism and interlocking institutions.

The theme of the book suggested the idea of taking that great symbol of freedom, the Statue of Liberty, and showing it exploited as a degraded and meaningless souvenir, a mass-manufactured miniature made of cheap metal and shipped to junk stores and tourist shops everywhere.

Because of budgetary restrictions, there was no four-color process available. Black plus a copper-colored metallic ink tint dropped over the statues was used instead. The budget did not allow for proofing, either. 3M Color Keys were used, and fingers were kept crossed.

Publisher: Delta Books (Dell Publishing Company, Inc.)
Art director: John Van Zwienen
Designer: Robert Anthony
Photographer: G. Janoff
Copywriter: Richard Kennedy

"I wish I'd written it."
—Robert C. Townsend, author of *Up The Organization*

America, Inc.

WHO OWNS AND OPERATES THE UNITED STATES

BY MORTON MINTZ AND JERRY S. COHEN

INTRODUCTION BY RALPH NADER

DELTA $2.95

Conoco's first big oil strike occurred at the "fabulous" 101 Ranch in Ponca City, Oklahoma. As a prelude to the company's upcoming centennial, Conoco, house magazine for Continental Oil Company, published a story on the historical event, "Memory of a Wild West Ranch."

Illustrator Alan Cober was commissioned to do the entire issue—25 illustrations in all, including four lead article illustrations. Each one was given its own individual character, to establish a pace, but all are identifiable as the work of the same illustrator.

The cover artwork on the 101 Ranch was chosen because it was the most colorful of all the illustrations submitted. The art director supplied Cober with a horseshoe and spike from the original ranch, which were incorporated into the artwork. A dark airbrush background was used to offset the line art and the type.

Publisher: Continental Oil Co.
Art director: Milt Simpson
Design firm: Johnson & Simpson, Newark, NJ
Designers: Milt Simpson, Gretchen Ackerman
Illustrator: Alan E. Cober
Copywriters: Maury Bates, R. Gaines, Hank Snelling

Illustrations from inside magazine.

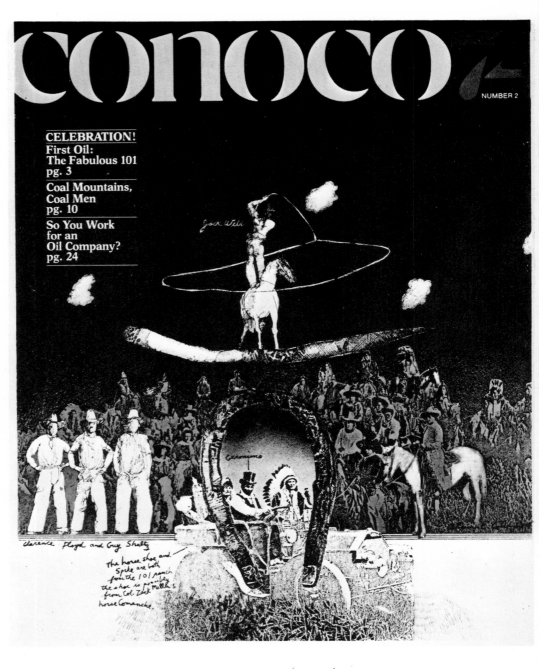

B